D1568517

THE OTHER SIDE

Growing Up Italian in America

THE OTHER SIDE

Growing Up Italian in America

by

Vincent Panella

Photographs by

Susan Sichel

Doubleday & Company, Inc.   Garden City, New York   1979

1. Theodore Roethke, "My Papa's Waltz," *The New Oxford Book of American Verse*, chosen and edited by Richard Ellmann, New York, Oxford University Press, 1976.

2. The quotation on page 62 is taken from *Beyond the Melting Pot*, by Nathan Glazer and Daniel Patrick Moynihan, M.I.T. Press, 1963.

3. "Across the Alley from the Alamo" was made popular by The Mills Brothers in the 1940s.

"My Papa's Waltz," copyright 1942 by Hearst Magazines, Inc., from *The Collected Poems of Theodore Roethke*. Reprinted by permission of Doubleday & Company, Inc., and Faber & Faber, Ltd.

Lyrics from "Across the Alley from the Alamo," by Joe Greene. Copyright 1947 by Michael Goldsen, Inc. Reprinted by permission of Michael Goldsen, Inc.

ISBN: 0-385-14733-3
Library of Congress Catalog Card Number 78-22346

Copyright © 1979 by Vincent Panella and Susan Sichel
All Rights Reserved
Printed in the United States of America
First Edition

ACKNOWLEDGMENTS

We want to thank all members of the Giaimo and Panella families who so generously gave us both the information and the photographs needed for this book. We also want to thank Marty Kelly for her valued opinions and spirited encouragement, Tracey Penton for his care in designing the book, and Karen Van Westering, our editor, for her support throughout.

For all our families

Vini with MOM + DAD   Oct. 1939

"Such waltzing was not easy."

Theodore Roethke,
"My Papa's Waltz"

THE OTHER SIDE

Growing Up Italian in America

Connections

As a boy I held my ears when my grandmother sang to me in Sicilian dialect. I was relieved that my non-Italian friends seemed indifferent to my grandparents' broken English. And although I could ascribe my family's habits and attitudes to being Italian, it would be many years until I understood what this meant. Later in life, when I sought self-understanding, I found in myself the best and worst of my family's values. I felt like Gulliver, waking up with the dawn and seeing the ropes which bound him.

I never knew they were country people. I'd never seen their tiny towns in southern Italy, beautiful, poor, serene, but for some, miserable. My family looked upon its origins with mixed emotions: bitterness, nostalgia, and a sense of lost values. Only my Sicilian grandfather seemed resolved about the change in his life. He spoke about his old home without remorse. He had escaped that poverty and isolation. He was having the last laugh.

These attitudes toward Italy were conveyed to my generation implicitly. Only later did I see that America was a choice for the older people, but not an absolute necessity. In Italy they might survive, but they would never prosper. So they came to the tenements with that wave of southern Italian immigrants in the early 1900s, the men unskilled, the women readily employable in the garment industry.

The transition to America consumed their energy. They had little time for the likes of me. I was third generation, ignorant of Italy, and too young to remember the Italian neighborhood we moved away from soon after I was born. I knew my family as city dwellers:

my grandfathers railroad workers; my father a city fireman, then bar owner, then real estate broker; my uncles paragons of my city heroes, physically tough men with a disposition to drink and gamble. Men I emulated when I was young, and envious of the tenement life I'd never known.

My family was too proud to advertise its struggle in America, and neither equipped nor inclined to articulate an identity to its children. We were Italian and different. Our special gifts and vulnerabilities, these I would discover on my own. I was to learn that my father was Neapolitan and my mother Sicilian, but I had no notion of these concepts as geographical and cultural. I sensed the discord between these two groups—it was more manifest in the women—but didn't realize until later that its roots reached back to Italian history. At our home in Queens my mother's family lived on the second floor, and we lived on the first. I was more of a companion to my mother's brothers than to my father: he always worked at two jobs. He came home late in the evening, and left early in the morning. Everyone was on the move. My grandfathers worked on the railroad together, my Sicilian grandmother constantly cooked and arbitrated, my father came and went as he pleased, my younger uncles were unruly.

Home was the place for meals and arguments. The meals were memorable, the arguments almost always over money. It was the hurdle they never cleared. At the table my father asked the price of everything we ate. He could always get it more cheaply, "downtown." Seeking his approval, my mother would present him with her purchases of food or clothing: he rarely extended praise. I learned his system of control very quickly: he never committed himself to a schedule the family could rely upon. And he always said we could do better. This kept us, using his expression, "on our toes."

We were a physical family. There was a good deal of kissing, hugging, slapping, ear twisting, and worse punishments for worse offenses. Disobedience was not tolerated. My father was the supreme authority, my mother a much weaker second-in-command. Neither was a companion with whom intimate fears or feelings could be shared. On those occasions when my father tried to engage me on such delicate subjects as sex and fighting, the circuits slowly shorted. He could not be an autocrat and an equal. My closest companion as a boy was my mother's youngest brother, Mario, an uncle who filled in for my often absent father, and who, without responsibility for my discipline, could be liberal with me. Mario introduced me to the world I wanted to know about—the world outside the house.

In time we became less Italian. The move from Hell's Kitchen to a non-Italian neighborhood in Queens was the major departure from the family's first culture. And our connection to Italy and family members there, once tightened by a chain of letters and packages, became tenuous. The packages slowed, then stopped. The letters became annual events, notes with the same phrases repeated year after year, notes cast aside quickly. We were here; they were there. English words crept into the language spoken at home and a kind of pidgin was used between first and second generations. Their dialect in its purer form was used as a way of concealing information from my generation. America was knocking at the door. The Progresso food salesman no longer came into our home when the supermarkets carried his products. An uncle married Irish; a sister married black; a cousin married Greek. The culture fractured and healed, fractured and healed, but always with the modification of the previous wound.

But I never knew my family completely. I'd grown up in a transition period, when we were shedding one culture and taking on another. I sensed that certain qualities were being lost, others retained or modified. I knew that in order to have a sense of my own identity I had to have a sense of theirs. I thought first of all about why my family built a new life in a new place. I learned that southern Italians were historically a class of migrant workers. While this fact made their passage to America explainable, it didn't shrink the dimension of their struggle. They came to America without skills, and without language, with the Latin roots of English buried deep under their dialect. On the Sicilian side, my family was illiterate in Italian. What could have been so miserable as to propel these ostensibly unequipped people so far from homes they'd held for centuries, homes they felt ambivalent about leaving? What had shaped them, who in turn had shaped me?

In 1976 I was living in an Iowa farmhouse and leading a patchwork life of writing, teaching, and raising chickens and cattle. It was in some ways a self-imposed exile from my family and its controlling pressures. But it was an exile which enabled me to think about them

15

while some of their pressures weren't operating. I took an opportunity to learn Italian at a nearby university, and that year traveled to Italy and the towns near Naples and Palermo where my family came from. I knew that whatever the narrow streets of those villages might hold, whatever insights or disappointments, I had to go. I had to make the connection denied by my family's inability to transmit its culture, denied by the circumstances of my growing up, and denied by my former lack of interest. Had I grown up like the previous generation, in a more completely Italian environment, my desire to know and possess a past might have been satisfied without making that trip.

I wanted a testament to my outlook on life. For as much as I'd once tried to deny them, these Italians had formed me. I was born of immigrants who never would have met in Italy: stoic Sicilians on my mother's side; witty, ambitious Neapolitans on my father's. I knew their double pull. Like a Sicilian peasant I could relax after physical work, wanting nothing more from life than a garden full of eggplants and tomatoes, a brace of Polled Herefords, and a few fancy roosters. But always, my contentment was interrupted by that Neapolitan gnawing which kept me awake at night and asked where the money was.

Being Italian

My parents, Grace Giaimo and Emilio Panella, met in the 1920s in that very Italian part of Manhattan known as Hell's Kitchen. They lived on opposite sides of West Thirty-third Street, on Tenth Avenue. My mother's was the only Sicilian family on a Neapolitan block. My father, his brother, and two sisters were late arrivals; the other Italians on the block called them *guineas* because of their broken English. I was never part of that neighborhood. My family moved to Jackson Heights, Queens, soon after I was born. But my sense of being Italian, with its frustrations and pleasures, has been the principal factor in my life, even when I wasn't conscious of it.

In Queens, nationality was a first point of reference. Jackson Heights was a neighborhood filled with Irish people, empty lots with poor soil and patches of grass or weeds, apartment houses of coarse, dark brick. Then the steam shovels came. The lots were dug up. Six-story buildings rose from the excavations. The Jewish people had arrived. There had always been few Italians in the neighborhood, and I remember my Sicilian grandfather traveling to Corona for his wine grapes and imported groceries.

I noticed the differences between us and them soon enough. Besides being a little poorer, we spoke a different language at home, a language remarked upon by my non-Italian friends, but never denigrated. My father and Sicilian grandfather, who jointly owned our private house, were fanatically frugal. My grandfather had an aversion to electricity which I didn't understand until I went to Europe. My friends were allowed the luxury of hamburgers for lunch at the Toddle House; my lunch always waited at home, along with admonitions against restaurant food: "It gives you *acida*!" Strange people came to our house, too: ladies in high black shoes who started loud arguments over what to name babies, a greasy, gold-toothed fellow who sold Progresso foods, and my grand-mother's half-brother and his wife. He owned a restaurant "down the village"; her hair was dyed red. On holidays they entertained us with mandolin and accordion. The song I remember most had a strange subject: the praise of mothers and codfish; everyone joined the chorus, singing in their alloyed Italian-American:

Oh Ma-Ma! Fish-a fish-a baccala!

The family rarely discussed these differences with the children. Everyone was busy, either working or assimilating. And perhaps they were too certain of their culture to think it could drown in the American swim. We were not American, not even Italian-American. We were to favor our family first, other Italians next. This was our concept of loyalty, and one prescription for growing up. Our job was not so much to become Americans as it was to be "moxie" and successful, like the Jewish people.

With few Italian influences outside the home, I stood at the perimeter of a mythical American culture, not a truly American one. I saw the Irish and Jewish diversity around me, but it never occurred to me that they too, especially the Jews, might feel equally on the outside. My job was to get *in*, to the place where I thought they were. And the first proving place was grammar school, where I found myself consistently failing the "breakfast test." This was an embarrassment concealed from my parents. During this test students were asked to stand and recite what they'd eaten for breakfast. True to European tradition my morning meal consisted of something to drink and a piece of Italian bread and butter. This was not the "balanced" diet displayed above every classroom blackboard of egg, cereal, juice, toast, and milk. I never discussed this with my family, not only because I didn't want to admit failing at school, but, more likely, I didn't think they were capable of dealing with American matters. After a while I learned to lie about what I ate.

I was intensely aware of our nationality and our habits. We were frugal, loud, and argumentative. And the older people spoke that funny language which they couldn't write down on paper for me.

Their dialect ran words together so tightly that phrases sounded like one word. By my sound and spelling we had an aunt named "Tubbapina." A crude, uncomfortable word which I wouldn't say. I dutifully lined up for my wet kiss but never uttered her name. Later I studied Italian and learned that *zia* meant *aunt*. "Tubbapina" was Zia Peppina, spoken very fast.

Our move to Queens isolated me not only from other Italians, but from my father's side of the family too, the Neapolitans. My contact with our full family was limited to some holiday dinners, funerals, and affairs called "football weddings," so named because the sandwiches were tossed around like footballs. But I couldn't give a family shape to that collection of relatives. Who were the stern men, the ladies in black? Who were the gorgeous younger women from Brooklyn and lower Manhattan? Where did they all fit in?

I grew up with my mother's side, the Sicilians. My grandmother was a strong, superstitious woman who passed on handy words like *sfatta* for overripe fruit, or *acida* for what bad food did to your stomach. I was too self-conscious to use their language with greater sophistication, and their impatient attempts to teach me yielded the numbers up to twenty and some other useful phrases. Once again, I shut my ears. I wanted to be American. I saw that their dialect tendency was to soften consonants and lengthen vowels: *gallone* was pronounced *galloona; sfatta, sfatha,* and so on. The only part of their language with currency for me was the profanity: most city boys knew that. I was selecting those parts of the culture which would pass inspection outside the home.

At the same time, I was never ashamed of being Italian. I was only aware of being different. After all, famous Italians had cracked the culture. And I was finding out that the "tougher men" in and around the neighborhood, those who congregated in gangs, those who fought in the Golden Gloves, were Italians. I saw them with their Tony Curtis hair, pegged pants, French-toed shoes. With them, there was an assumed connection.

My family called Italy "the other side." The phrase was an increment of their Americanization. But Italy to me was that collection of relatives, the source of that slurried language, the destination of CARE packages, the difference between my friends and myself. I saw it also in epiphanies: my father, a man not given to displays of emotion, once drank too much and sang the wedding song about the young woman who, seeing the moon over the ocean, implores her mother to find her a husband. Or my father again, visiting me in Maryland and seeing a walnut tree near my house: here the man who could pressure merchants into selling anything from nails to used cars at a lower price, the man who scorned all activity not related to cash, exclaimed with an innocence so rare for him, "We have these trees in Italy!" as he filled the pockets of his unpressed suit with nuts. Then collecting himself, he looked around at the poor white country where I'd chosen to live and said, "The country's the same, no matter where you are."

We bought a summer place in a development where the cabins were as close together as the houses in Queens. The small, creosoted cabins had been built on a mountain, walking distance from fields and farms. On my Sicilian grandmother's first visit she took a knife and began cutting some of the young dandelion plants growing around the house while I looked on, embarrassed that people might walk by and think us too different. She called it *cicoria*. She boiled it, then sautéed it in garlic and olive oil. It was strong and slightly bitter. "Eat!" she said. "Is good for your blood!" With a gay print cloth tied around her head she hiked to the cow pasture and picked buckets of berries, unafraid, as we children were, of the fictional bull roaming with the cows. She even made my father drive her to the farm where she bought raw milk and drank it warm. To all of us, Petrina Giaimo embodied everything Italian. She was a big, strong woman, black haired, blue-eyed, with a sense of humor to offset her husband's resignation, an ability to guide the family through and around tragedy, and an Italian remedy for every ailment. She was full of stories, about Italy, about her Tenth Avenue days. While she rested in the hospital after giving birth to twins, a doctor squeezed some milk from her breast, tasted it, and gave her a third child to nurse.

Emilio Panella and Grace Giaimo Panella

Wedding   Manhattan, 1936

GRACE +EMILIO

1937

1938

The Giaimo home   Queens, 1941   Emilio   194

Queens, 1951

The Panella family   Queens, 1954

The Italian Boy

Being Italian in America allowed me to choose from two worlds. At first I took the male image, the menu, the habit of making everything a secret. I rejected the socially unacceptable parts: the language, the family history, the old culture. I also rejected overt attempts by other Italians to establish rapport with me by mentioning nationality. I wanted such connections implicit, cool, gangsterish. I was also content to embody most of the prejudices held toward Italians, and would have adopted more if I'd been able. These included taking advantage of female romantic notions, and, when possible, bullying other males who were victims of their own ignorance. Like many Italian boys, I was proud of the gangster image. This was my secret feather. After all, these men had all the marbles: brains, brawn, the law in their pockets, and all the money. I romanticized my future as a benign gangster, tough, slick, highly educated, education being the latest marble.

I was let down by the reluctant conclusion that none in my family were racketeers (racketeers was our word, rarely mafia). I observed my grandfathers' monotonous lives, how they worked every day at the uptown railroad yard, and how they walked home from the subway station at exactly the same time. My Neapolitan grandfather was a plumber; the Sicilian did what we called "pick and shovel." Over the years I watched my father catapult out of bed with the 6 A.M. alarm, walking in a dazed circle around the room before getting into the pants which my mother had often rifled while he slept. The act was too good for the rackets. But I didn't abandon the dream so easily. My father, after all, was a man of few visible pleasures. And how often had he taken me into Manhattan, told me to wait in the car, and returned an hour or so later, finding me hunched up against the cold, head retracted like a turtle's into my coat. What had he been doing? When I asked, he mumbled or changed the subject. But certainly, more than anyone in my family, he was capable of surprise. Maybe someday, I thought, perhaps when I was twenty-one, he would lead me into the secret room and introduce me to the tough men in dark suits who would swear a fealty to me in broken English as romantic as the hand-kissing scene in *The Godfather*.

I eventually grasped the reality. My father was an ex-fireman who owned a bar on South Street and worked at real estate in Queens. None of my schoolyard enemies mysteriously disappeared or suddenly showed up for stickball in bandages. None of my father's friends waited for me in the shadows like black angels and told me how to solve my problems. I was the son of a workingman whose control of the family was absolute, dictatorial. His way was the right way and the only way. Like his father, he was feared. Like his father, he didn't reveal his emotions. He was secretive about his movements. At family gatherings he was almost always the last to arrive. At home his hours were irregular and unpredictable. He was the unknown in the family equation and this was his way of controlling it. I would have to find other outlets for my romantic tendencies.

Outside the home I was learning about the Irish and Jewish. I didn't know what my father knew: that my interaction with these groups was inevitable, and that all of us had started in Manhattan a few generations ago. In Jackson Heights the Irish were the dominant force. The Catholic church was an Irish bastion, from the strict priests and nuns down to the rowdy students who formed the neighborhood gang I would eventually join. The public school was the catch basin for the rest of us, Jews and Eastern Europeans, a few Italians, and the few Irish who didn't attend Catholic school. The Jewish boys were smart in school but averse to fighting. The Irish didn't like them. I found myself painfully and miserably drawn to both groups, comfortable with Jewish warmth and verbal interplay, but wanting male approval on my own terms, and the social acceptance which I didn't get at home.

The Irish were more visible. They filled the church during the children's Mass, they galloped through the neighborhood like cowboys, they wore pegged pants and porkpie hats. Before my thirteenth year they asked me to join them, and I knew the decision would mean a new pattern for my life. I would have to reject my Jewish friends for a rowdy bunch, and that choice meant compromise. The gang offered security, and a promise to navigate the seas outside the house more forcefully. But they also represented ignorance and parochialism. I agonized, but I joined: their way of life was more in line with my illusions.

Unaware of such adolescent ordeals, my family asked only that I observe their rules for physical confinement. I was to attend school, do my homework, and come home on time. The matrix of our intimacy was physical. But they couldn't watch me all the time. My fantasy of being the arch-Italian male was a nugget in my pocket growing large. But as I tested myself in the streets this dream intersected reality with quixotic precision. With much misery I proved not to be the fearless equal to my uncles and father. The nugget became heavy and distorted. It would have to be shaved. My disappointments only intensified my differences. I was aware of a special footing, somewhere between the Jewish and Irish, and somewhere between my unconfident mother and my iron father. To make this zone livable, I escaped into books.

Vincent Panella   Vermont, 1978

Emilio Panella   Newburgh, New York, 1977

VIN + DAD — 1939

Father and Son

"What kind of book is that?"

"A novel."

"Why are you reading it?"

"Because I like it."

"Can you make money reading that book?"

"What do you mean?"

"Just what I said. Will you get paid if you read the book? And if not, is there something in the book that tells you how to make money, or that somehow leads to money?"

"I don't know."

"Then why are you reading that book?"

Falling by the Wayside

My father had a politician's ability to use a cliché. He pushed me through high school and college on one slogan. The lazy and misdirected were bound to "fall by the wayside." His pep talks, rife with the phrase, occurred at least once a week. He relentlessly repeated the theme that education meant money and dignity, the last inversely proportional to the manual work a man had to do. The setting for these talks was the front room of our first-floor apartment, the television room, many-windowed, hermetically sealed from the rest of the house by heavy french doors. When I entered the house and he was home, he'd say, "Vincent, I want to talk to you," as if the gravest business were at hand. We'd retire to the front room and the door would close, opening only for my mother, obediently bringing the demitasse, happy that despite his frequent absence he was home at last and shaping the family.

I didn't realize it then, but the business was serious. The purpose of those talks was to protect his part of our bargain; probably the most important bargain I would make; a bargain with results neither of us could predict. At thirteen I'd made him a promise: to finish high school and go to college in exchange for a private room in our apartment, a room I could lock, a room allowing me the privacy of study and the luxury of my moods; a room for the only son, whose three sisters would have to share a room. He offered me this privacy to protect my future, and to protect me from outside influences, namely those rowdy, brawling, and drinking boys—mostly Irish— who'd become my companions. These boys went to the "local" high school. I went to Brooklyn Tech. At their school they could play hooky for weeks at a time and be forgiven. My father knew this. He knew the pattern of their lives: that they would quit school and perhaps influence me to do the same.

So I kept my promise. I locked the door of the bedroom and brought home the grades. But in that room I became a reader and a dreamer. I became what my father would later call "A Peculiar Individual," who didn't consider money a primary value. After doing my homework I'd stare out the window like a feverish swain, conjuring my sensual future. Or I'd read novels, mostly pulp ones, and most of these in that nice category called "historical fiction." My private world rang with Heroes and Gods. I'd started with Homer and, unguided in my reading, continued to whatever derivative fiction could feed my private obsessions. I was building a retreat, not only from the monotony and disappointments of my life, but, less consciously, from the world my father was guiding me toward, the career which, in my ignorance and isolation, seemed appropriate enough. Like many Italian immigrant sons, I would become an engineer.

I was bound to this profession not just by his tireless indoctrination on the meaning of Sputnik for my bank account. It became clear later on that I was bound by a guilt of our mutual and unconscious creation, guilt rooted in the family symbol of sacrifice; guilt rooted in the substance my family related to all tangible and sometimes intangible matter; guilt, in short, rooted in money. My father's main occupation had always been bars. And I'd seen enough of them, and worked long enough in one of them, to realize that my college dollars were earned in the taxing drudgery of that business: drunks, corrupt police, a neglected family, the half-dozen broken noses he'd picked up in the bars he owned from Harlem to South Ferry and back up the river to Newburgh, the location of his last bar, where I worked. During the summers and holidays of my college years we worked the bar together, eight to four in the morning, sleeping in shifts on a cot upstairs, and eating breakfast in a diner while the sun came up.

By the end of my sophomore year at Carnegie Tech I found myself with two problems, and my father was the adversary in each. I wanted to quit engineering because I knew where it would lead me—to a steel plant or a missile mill—places I'd seen or read about, places which would stress the kind of conformity which I knew was a threat. I didn't want it. But I didn't know how to tell him. I was halfway through engineering school by then. The cost had been five thousand dollars and I knew where the money was coming from.

Something else was happening that summer. My parents were going through a crisis which would lead to their permanent separation. It was partly the difference in their backgrounds—two clannish yet diverse cultures in opposition—which led to the break. It was partly a matter of what we then called "incompatibility." My father was dominant and uncommunicative; my mother was raised as an Old World Italian. Her husband didn't operate in that world. I was drawn to my mother's side, perhaps because of loyalties to the Sicilians, who'd always been closer; perhaps because I was the only son. But I fell into it. Relatives had whispered in my ear. The engineer had seen the data, not all of it, but enough.

My sullen manner behind the bar told my father that something was wrong, but neither of us was very good at bringing out emotions. The school news, I knew, would hurt him; my sentiments toward my mother would surely anger him. I thought about how many times we'd talked about school. He'd always close the discussion by asking me for the final commitment, the one I was most unwilling to make: "But Vincent, do you *like* this metallurgical engineering?" And I would say, "It's okay," like a reticent teen-ager, hoping he'd read me as well as he read his customers.

At nineteen I wasn't sophisticated enough to leave my parents to their private affairs. I hadn't been raised to leave any family member to his or her private affairs. And I desired to protect my mother not only by reason of right and wrong, but because I resented the man trying to mold my life. But guilt constrained me, guilt for my father's disappointment in the only male Panella in college, who didn't know why he was there, and guilt for five thousand dollars in what the family called "blood money" because it came so hard in the bar.

Why did I feel guilty for wanting to set my life on its natural course? Because I was new to choice, and afraid of it. It was easier then to blame my reluctance to act on the money. My father and I were trapped, he in the no longer tenable conception that a well-salaried job with shirt and tie meant happiness; myself in the equally shaky position that his manner of making money was so painful that I should defer to it. But such considerations were under the surface that summer. He didn't say, "I send you to college with this blood money." I didn't say, "I feel guilty about spending it on something I don't like." There had never been much two-way discussion between us. My father's natural desire, true to his upbringing, was to exert unquestioned authority over his wife and children. He enforced this authority by violence whenever necessary, and by unflagging salesmanship, always. My happiness lay in his direction, not my own.

This was the inevitable struggle between us, heightened by the focus on money, guilt, and fear. What had become new in my life to precipitate the struggle was the notion of self-satisfaction: that somewhere, somehow, there existed labor which would pay me and satisfy me simultaneously. This desire was foreign and indulgent to a man who grew up in a West Side tenement during the Depression.

During the summer of my nineteenth year I had the will for a battle. A few weeks before my junior year began, another school offered to enroll me in its English program. I told my father about it. During the same discussion I defended my mother to him, accusing him of neglecting family duty. Double crisis, double resolution. He fired me from the bar and gave me a choice: an engineering degree or none at all.

Then something happened to simplify my decision. Soon after our argument there was trouble in the bar. My father threw a customer out. After closing time the same night, while my father was counting out the register, the customer threw a beer bottle from outside the door. The bottle struck the bar mirror and the shower of glass brought the tally of broken noses to six. I went back to work without being asked. And with a bandage over his nose that looked like a coffee cup he handed me my tuition check and I went back to school.

That year I fell in love with The American Girl of My Dreams. Did I see her that way? Love can be an intense illusion. We would later marry and divorce. But within the woman I loved was the America I wanted to discover. She came from a small town in Pennsylvania. Her father was a country doctor, a sensitive, sentimental man who loved fishing and skeet shooting. He made house calls late at night and was as much a psychologist as a general practitioner. He might have stepped from the cover of *The Saturday Evening Post*, aware of the intensified image, but proud to embody it.

40

Being in love with his daughter steadied me, and an education in engineering was easier to bear.

I was still, however, operating under a strongly felt but unarticulated family influence. I sensed that I had to be on my own to even identify that influence, so after graduation I put miles between myself and my family. I worked in California for a missile company, quit when it became unbearable, roamed a little, wrote a little, and tried to get some idea of what lay between the American coasts. When news reached my father that I'd quit my job he labeled me "The Family Screwball" and went about his business. I enjoyed my independence. I would never be an engineer again, I thought, even if it had cost him ten thousand dollars. I would never end up with my picture on the cover of *Forbes Magazine*, a man who invented a gadget and rode it to control of a company.

But I only *thought* I was free of my family. The Girl of My Dreams grew impatient in the wings while I roamed. We married. I found work as a technical writer. The pay was poor. So I gave engineering a final try, this time with a smaller company, this time thinking only of the money. In 1963, after less than a year on the job, I looked upon the draft as a means of rescue. Two years later I came out of the Army with an unsalable first novel which avoided or blurred most of the important forces in my life. There was a child. I was twenty-five. Engineering was out. The GI Bill came along and I used it to get a degree in English. My father tried to dissuade me with the old medicine: marathon lectures. This time I had the strength to resist him. So did my wife. We packed our Volkswagen. On the day we left for Penn State he stood by the car, looked at the baby tucked behind the back seat, and said, "I should have made you a lawyer." When he saw the look on my face he realized what he'd said. Finally, I thought to myself, there is some progress.

But we break away slowly. In the years which followed, I seemed more in the grip of my past than ever. At twenty-nine, with responsibilities as husband, father of two children, part-time teacher, part-time graduate student, I simply substituted new guilts for old. I wasn't writing. I wasn't making money. I wasn't doing well enough as father, teacher, or husband. I had the habit of guilt, that southern Italian addiction to disaster and pessimism. And unless I broke free, I would do nothing well.

41

Vincent Paul Panella

Manhattan, 1941

Queens, 194

First Holy Communion   Queens, 1947

ENGINEERING — Vincent Paul Panella of Rt. 94, Newburgh, has received a bachelor of science degree in metallurgical engineering from Carnegie Institute of Technology. He is the son of Emilio and Grace Panella of New Windsor. He was graduated from Brooklyn Technical High School at Brooklyn in 1957, and is a former resident of Mt. Lodge Park.'

1961

1963

Wedding   Queens, 1962

Distance

I left home for college at seventeen and for many years afterward lived as far from my family as possible. Especially later in life, this was done in a spirit of exile, knowing my father disparaged me; knowing my mother needed me; and knowing her brothers had stepped in to protect her from my father. These uncles, so close to me as a youngster, expected me to take my mother's side.

But I felt a special responsibility to break the pattern of living near family, the pattern so prevalent in the generation before me, and in my own. Making my own life was a psychological necessity. I reasoned that the risk of staying near home would be to clash with and alienate those I loved. Later I would discover this reasoning false: I acknowledged that love was stronger than my family's more taxing habits, and that we could live with each other on our own terms: I simply had to fight for that right. But as a young man I hadn't developed the strength to try that battle. It was easier to leave the field and grumble about their oppressiveness.

A cousin once told me, "You were lucky, you escaped." From what? From expectations and controls. Had I lived close to home I would have had to explain everything, to justify everything, from my taste in shoes to my taste in friends. What bothered me most of all was that these expectations often had little to do with my ideas or values. They were simple and numerous oppressions, a fixation with concrete actions. Was I taking the subway downtown? Why not the bus? Was I buying tires or a battery for my car? Where? Why not *there*? Everything was questioned. And there was a blind impulse to chop, curb, or redirect any activity which I might do independently.

My family wanted me home, and they wanted to see the tangible fruits of my education, the money and clothes, the expensive car. And when I didn't display them, they wanted to know why a man with so much education and seeming intelligence wasn't a success as they defined it. Their generation, and most of my own, had become firmly fixed in the blue collar class. Some worked for the city of New York. They had security and benefits. I was patching together a motley career as an engineer, teacher, writer, bartender, and newspaper reporter. In their sense of the term I wasn't employed. So I stayed away from home in order to love them.

There was more than enough to keep me away. The 1960s were a bad time for my family. My older sister's marriage had broken up. My marriage had broken up. My mother and father had separated for the second time. This last circumstance was especially painful for my mother, who saw the separation as publicly embarrassing. She and my father were living in a community populated heavily by Italian-Americans in upstate New York, and after their separation my father began living with another woman in the same community. Neither of them would file for divorce. My mother had been reared for a single pattern of life, and she preferred a marriage on paper to a divorce in fact. My father, knowing her position, preferred to retain his options. Both tried to draw their children into the resultant feud over support money and visiting policies by testing our loyalties. My mother forbade us to visit our father in his house; he was hurt by our loyalties to her. The atmosphere was tense with lies, evasions, and all-out battles with both our parents for our freedom of choice.

I was torn between what I conceived as my responsibility toward my own growth and my responsibility toward my parents. I wanted them to solve their problem. Yet I knew that aunts and uncles on both sides of the family were pointing to me as the only son who should step in between his outraged parents. What I really felt, but would never admit to anyone, was that I was still tied to their standard of material success. Without it, I thought, my character had no force. And having nothing to show for life on their terms, I couldn't exert influence with either parent.

Confining myself to visits, I saw that little had changed at home. In the kitchen my aunt and mother argued over how to make coffee or whether to season the spaghetti sauce with oregano. I drove with

48

my father and he told me to stop for red lights. Nothing is done alone, unless one overcomes their tendency to control. This is the strongest manifestation of the old culture. The need for that protective love was created in another time, in another country. And yet I saw those qualities in myself, mitigated or made latent by the separation I chose to make from them. In my own marriage I saw my father's patterns: a reticence to articulate emotion, an unwillingness to make commitments on any scale, a brooding inwardness which expected my wife to divine my feelings. I had a penchant for the grudge, an intolerance toward new people and ideas, and that Italian proclivity for being obsessed with the concrete at the expense of the abstract.

But there were other qualities in my family which time and distance couldn't change. No matter how long my absences, and some lasted several years, I was immediately taken back into the family when I came home. The table was set, we sat down to eat and drink, and the years and miles made no difference at all. Food was the vehicle of our immediate intimacy. My mother—living alone since her separation—carried the dishes in from the kitchen: stuffed mushrooms, eggplant parmigiana ("My eggplant won't give you heartburn!"), a tray of lasagne, broccoli steamed with garlic and flavored with fresh lemon, and *chicoria*, now a delicacy. My uncle Mario, always on hand when I came home, would, like his father, place the gallon of wine on the floor beside his chair; by controlling the wine, he'd hope to control the conversation. My sisters teased me about my mother's favoritism: "Vincent! When she heard you were coming she cooked for three days!"

But that distance gave me perspective on them. I saw over the years a lack of development in my family's outlook and way of life. They seemed not so much discontent with their lot as unable or unwilling to move beyond it; as if in over-all potential they were stalled, on one hand in the economically constricted middle class, on the other in the psychology of a southern Italy which they'd never seen. Most of my generation and the one before it are bound by that narrow, village outlook: disinterested in politics, cognizant of higher education as a path to a job, not a sensibility, and lacking confidence in their own ability to change things.

Our strong family cohesion also showed signs of weakening. Cousins lost contact as they moved to the suburbs. Younger generations knew little about their heritage. And after my parents' separation those Sicilians and Neapolitans who'd been neighbors on West Thirty-third Street weren't talking. At funerals they arranged to miss each other. At weddings they occupied different tables or didn't attend if the opposition was present. Between Neapolitan and Sicilian the old rent was still there, especially among the older generation. It seemed as if the worst aspects of the old culture had thrived in America.

During my long absence I still played Hamlet to their ghosts, my tortured ear at the long distance wire, hearing the reports of my father's offenses, my mother's stubborn pride, or the latest sacrilege of a wayward brother-in-law. And like Hamlet, I puzzled how to answer those deeds. For six years I lived in an Iowa farmhouse— owning a Pontiac and a pickup truck as manifests of my duality— and wrote a fiction based on my family and stilted by my ignorance of the material. I dreamt that someday I'd return to the city with those Hollywood checks, and, like Sinatra, have it both ways: theirs and mine.

But distance can't cut cultural ties. In Iowa I'd placed myself in the midst of a culture which seemed nondescript enough to provide the lack of distraction I needed for my work. I was living in a hundred-twenty-year-old farmhouse, a dilapidated clapboard creature built box by box to accommodate the Irish immigrants who settled there after the Great Potato Famine. My landlord was second generation, a man my father's age, a man who considered himself Irish but who knew no details about his family's origins or the interaction between the Irish and other immigrant groups in America. Yet I was surprised at the currency he placed on his Irishness. That part of Iowa was almost all Irish, a region of small farms and relatively late settlers who took second pick after the Germans.

One bleak Sunday while simmering a pot of tomato sauce I saw my landlord and a small group of men pulling an Angus cow in from the fields with a pickup truck. They tied the moaning creature inside a shed and began to abort it: its calf had breach-formed and died in the womb. I went outside to watch, standing in the bitter wind while they worked, reaching deep into the cow's stomach to pull out the putrid, rotting pieces, using ropes, cables, and even a jack to remove the head and rib cage. The landlord stood politely amused at my city curiosity: "Hell, this ain't nothin'." When they

50

were finished, the unburdened cow lumbered into the darkening fields, bellowing for its own kind. The remains of the calf were left for rats and raccoons.

It was a miserable day, more miserable because it should have been spring; a cold, dark day with the unchecked wind throttling the soybean stubble. I thought about where and how America had carried the Italians and Irish. In New York the Irish had almost driven my family back to Italy. Here was an Irishman who knew nothing about that, an Irishman who had his own struggle. Yet he was such a distant Irishman, unsure and not really concerned about his parents' and grandparents' origins in Ireland. He knew less about his original culture than I did about mine, yet in those bleak Iowa fields he clung to it more.

Inside the warm farmhouse that day I poured some tomato sauce over a plate of ziti and wondered about my own connections. I'd spent my life denying or ignoring them, the strongest forces in my life, refusing to understand my background because it hadn't been explained to me, and because its manifestations in America had been reduced, largely, to pizza, mafia, Hollywood distortion, or the set of adolescent cliches I once embraced. The influence my family exerted on me was immune to distance. And my desire to know them had been buried for too long by my frustration with those traits I considered old-world and retrograde.

The Family

When they talk about their early days in America, both sides gloss over certain events: their brushes with the law, their contact with gangsters, and to a degree their sources of income. This is to be understood. They were new to an alien place, and they had to scuffle. Besides, southern Italians are usually secretive, even to inquiring family members. Some of my questions were answered with blank stares, or those mannered shoulder shrugs.

My father's side originated in a suburb of Benevento, a city east of Naples known today for its manufacture of Strega, a *liquore*, and *torrone*, a nougat candy. Benevento is the capital of its province, and was distinguished in Roman times as a crossroad of the Appian Way, and in the sixth century as the headquarters for the Lombard duchy in southern Italy.

The four Panella brothers who arrived here at the turn of the century were unskilled laborers; but unlike the Sicilian side of my family they could read and write. They believed in education and, to a degree, the arts. Two played the mandolin, and all of them knew opera through the minstrels who passed through their one-street town in the Apennines and sang the famous arias. A fifth brother remained in Italy. He was my father's namesake and a Jesuit; he died at twenty-four, enfeebled, they say, from a life of study and isolation. I was surprised to learn about him: my habit had always been to lump my relatives together in a single, uneducated mass.

The brothers left their tiny house and plot of land in their parents' hands and came here, not so much to escape misery, but to seek their fortunes. Pasquale and Vincenzo came first, paving the way for Enrico and Giuseppe. Pasquale, the oldest, was a strong, stern man who soon became a foreman on the New York Central Railroad. Vincenzo and the others tried several lines of work. They opened bars and grocery stores, usually as partners. They peddled cheese, wine, harmonicas brought from Italy, even pistols. For a few years they raised fruit and chickens on a rented farm in Connecticut. None of their enterprises lasted. They are remembered as too hotheaded for the retail business, and too eager to pursue new opportunities. Vincenzo and Giuseppe ultimately settled for blue collar jobs, the former with the railroad, the latter with the city subway system. Enrico, whose activities are most poorly remembered by the family, returned to Italy after a few years. There is an overtone of trouble associated with his departure, but none in my family knows exactly why he left. In Italy he resumed his former occupation as a *carabiniere*. He inherited the family property, where his descendants live today.

During his early years in America my grandfather ran a tavern on Tenth Avenue, somewhere in the Thirties, the exact location forgotten by my family. From all accounts, the brothers were closely knit, never hesitating to help each other out, and making their money both inside and outside the law, as was common in those days. Pasquale was perhaps the most influential of the four, able to get railroad work for his brothers, and able to help them out of trouble through his connections. If the Panella brothers had a common characteristic, it wasn't the drive to make money, but the ability to spend it. They ate and drank well, and they bought expensive goods—traits passed on to most of their descendants. The history of this family in America during their first two generations contains plot and subplot, underworld figures, years unaccounted for or conveniently forgotten, and an occasional corpse. This was consistent with their nature. The brothers were in the main tough and ambitious. More importantly, they were accustomed to having their own way. They sometimes got in over their heads, however; this allowed them to exercise their appetite for drama, a trait also seen in future generations.

But the other side of my family, the Sicilians, were the timeless and steady creatures of the earth. They didn't know the meaning of big-time dreams, at least the first generation didn't. My grandparents, Pietro Giaimo and Petrina Bruno, came from the Sicilian mountains. When a racketeer whose hometown was near my grandmother's tried to court her, she returned to Italy, in fear. She came back to America only when certain he was no longer interested. Then she resumed her career as a dress finisher in a Jewish-owned sweatshop. She was a superstitious woman, believing in witches, the evil eye, olive oil as the universal cure and the reason I never had acne, all the Sicilian folklore. She fed the birds because she believed they were the souls of the dead. She married, after some deliberation, the man whose home was a few steps from her own in Italy. Pietro came here in 1910 to escape his poverty. He found his first years in America so difficult and depressing that he almost went back to his poor village. He wasn't used to the pace of work in America. His construction job cut his hands and ruined his clothing and shoes, of which he had too few. But soon he found more suitable work, in a bakery. Then he married and started his own bakery, in the cellar of his tenement. He made a regular life with few surprises. From Tenth Avenue he moved to Queens. Two of his sons bought homes nearby. A divorced daughter, Katie, lived with him. Until he died, he was the hub of the wheel.

Since I grew up closer to the Sicilians, I know the sound of their dialect, even though I could never speak it. I knew the simple rhythm of my grandfather's life: work, food, rest, paychecks. His sons teased him because he could remember a twenty-year-old electric bill. He suffered the condescension of other Italians because of his rural dialect, legendary frugality, and backward Sicilian ways. In the days when they were on speaking terms my father tried to convince him to invest in real estate. He could have bought a block's worth of stores in Queens for ten thousand dollars. He could have bought their tenement on West Thirty-third Street for about the same price. His only financial gamble was to put several thousand dollars in the Italian bank. He lost almost all of it when Mussolini devalued the currency. This was a great and tragic lesson in his life, and it put an end to any financial experiment. It was his nature not to change. He came from an isolated village, a village which, except for a few motorbikes and tiny cars buzzing through its tunnel-like streets today, hasn't changed since the days of the Arabs and Norman French.

I wasn't aware of the differences between them at first. They were all Italians, people who didn't match the Americans, people whose language and obsessions were at variance with the world I was trying to enter. I would know the Neapolitans less intimately. My grandmother on that side died long before I was born. My grandfather died when I was five. My Neapolitan aunts and uncles lived in Brooklyn and other parts of Queens, and I didn't see them as often as I did the Sicilians, who shared our house in Jackson Heights.

Slowly I would learn that the Neapolitans, in obvious ways more sophisticated, could often be less tolerant than my mother's side of the family. Perhaps this was because they took up my father's causes, and perhaps because they inherited the Panellas' nervous and idealistic pride. They were averse to uncertainty, strong-willed, vocal, and physical, insisting on loyalty and able to take revenge when it wasn't given. It was the Sicilians who more easily forgave the transgressions of my generation. Maybe such forbearance was rooted in their culture. But more likely it was a product of my grandmother's knowledge—never explicitly stated—that America was changing us. Her will to hold us together was strong.

From their point of view they may be an unspectacular family, typically southern Italian, with a predictable track of emigration from rural Italy to the east coast of America. But they captured my imagination because I knew them so impressionistically, and because my understanding of them was restricted by their language and habits.

The Bread Business

In a tenement on West Thirty-third Street and Tenth Avenue, Petrina and Pietro Giaimo raised the second generation on my Sicilian side: my uncles Angelo, Willie, and Mario, my aunt Katie, and my mother, Grace. This building was also the site of the bread business which the family operated for twenty-eight years. It is the last standing tenement on the street where my parents met, a three-story walk-up with an all-important stoop once used as a gathering place, and a roof where women sunned themselves and posed for pictures in Betty Grable style. Today the frontage of the building has been painted over, but the rest of its exterior, exposed as adjacent tenements were torn down, is scarred, distorted, and starting to crumble. Next door on the Tenth Avenue side is a new McDonald's, its twin golden arches an acrylic shock to the area, its parking lot stretching to Thirty-fourth Street like a band of licorice. No symbol of time passing in America could be more fitting, no juxtaposition of values more discordant. The other buildings on the block—including my father's across the street—have been leveled and replaced, mostly with low-slung, well-secured warehouses. The view from Tenth Avenue is clear to the Jersey palisades. This is an unpeopled neighborhood, a trucking zone, in an urban sense fallow and unused. The city may build a four-block convention center between West Thirty-fourth and Thirty-eighth Streets. If the center is built, the last trace of my parents' and grandparents' first community in America will disappear. Even now it's hard to imagine this area as a crowded, almost exclusively Italian neighborhood, in the days of hard manual work and arranged marriages between immigrants lonely for home, the streets filled with darkly dressed people, and colored by railroad cars and vegetable stands.

My uncles speak about "them days" on Tenth Avenue with more pleasure and pride than bitterness. But I wasn't curious about their life there until later, when I realized that the West Side was America's proving ground for Italians like those in my family. I once thought of my grandparents, especially the Sicilians, as rather mindless occupants of America, people who somehow got here and simply went to work. Much of this impression was caused by my inability to speak with them. When they slipped into dialect with their fellow Sicilians, I sensed a degree of sophistication which I could never share, and so I paid little mind to it.

When I became more interested in my family, their act of immigration became a great puzzle. These were illiterate people from the Sicilian mountains, people who would never travel the hundred kilometers to Palermo unless to leave the country, people who immigrated to the largest city in a country where they couldn't speak the language. Where did they get the nerve? How could Italy have been so miserable when they sang songs about it and clung so hard to it? I found one answer in the history of migrating Italian laborers. As Italy lost its ability to support its population—and southern Italy was especially impoverished—Italians traveled to those parts of the world where their skills had value. In the late nineteenth and early twentieth centuries Italians worked and settled in Western Europe, North Africa, South America, and the United States. In America their immigration coincided, quite naturally, with a growing textile and construction industry. For Italian women like Petrina, the marketable skill was sewing. For Italian men, there was a market for unskilled labor.

There were other characteristics of the Italian immigration to America at the turn of the century. It was primarily southern Italian, and these Italians, more than any other immigrant group in America, had little intention of staying here. My Sicilian grandparents were typical in this respect. Their plan was to bring their family here, make as much money as they could, and return home. But as they put down roots and discovered they were going to stay, they looked back to Italy with a mixture of bitterness and nostalgia. Italy had everything but work. They knew the bargain they'd struck.

Something else explains why such people would leave their backward towns. Their immigration built on an already established Italian population to smooth the transition. Thus Petrina, a two-time immigrant, came to America in 1906 and was taken in by her aunt, a woman who functioned as a mother to the seventeen-year-old girl. Their living and working environment in lower Manhattan was almost as "Italian" as home. "Petrinedda," her dialect name, found work at once in a sweatshop on Hester Street, and she would have stayed in America indefinitely if it hadn't been for an incident with a man, an incident believable only when one realizes that in the early days the small-town outlook was preserved in New York City.

She was sharing an apartment on Eldridge Street with her aunt and cousin, people from her hometown. A man was calling on her cousin. He was not only Sicilian: his native *paese* of Gangi was a neighboring town to my grandmother's. He had that solemn, male arrogance which assumed that any woman he wanted couldn't refuse him. But the frightening part about this man to Petrina was his reputation of being "mafia," something more fearful to her than the evil eye. This man arrived at the apartment one night with a box of *cannoli*. He sat in the living room with Petrina and her cousin. At a certain point the cousin left the room. The man made a proposition to Petrina. The incident so mortified her that she flushed her *cannoli* down the toilet after pretending to eat it. Then she returned to Italy, and remained there until certain the man had other interests. This turned out to be five years.

She returned in 1913. Again she found work in the sweatshop. Then a girlfriend from home arranged a meeting with her brother, Pietro Giaimo, a baker, a man she already knew, a man she considered acceptable but uninteresting. She considered his proposal for two weeks before accepting. Pietro was then a three-way partner in a bakery. The new couple took a second-story apartment in the building on Thirty-third and Tenth, and their rent included the use of a large brick oven in the basement. With this oven, Pietro started an independently owned bread business which was to last until 1942.

As the couple settled into family life and earned a regular income, they sent for relatives. Pietro sent for the older of his two brothers; the youngest, Vittorio, remained in Sicily to look after the house and parents. With Petrina's help her father, brother, stepmother, and stepbrother also came to New York. Mamma Grande, as the stepmother was called, was a tough, wiry woman who found

61

work in the dressmaking industry at once. Her husband, Vito, a man given to much drink and little labor, held various temporary jobs, mostly as a street sweeper. But he swore never to die in America, and in 1924 he returned to the Bruno house in Sicily, which was being kept by his younger son, Leonardo. Mamma Grande chose to stay behind with her son, who eventually opened a restaurant in Greenwich Village called Bruno's, a restaurant which lasted until the 1950s. As Pietro and Petrina built their family and their bread business in America, they maintained their connections with Sicily, sending money home until their tiny houses were secure in their families' hands.

They were the only Sicilians on a Neapolitan block and they took their teasing (about being gangsters and carrying knives) without malice. Petrina was a big, motherly woman, impervious to ethnic slurs from Italians and non-Italians alike. She was our strongest family figure, joker, samaritan, and something of a surrogate mother to the semi-orphaned Neapolitan boy across the street, Emilio Panella. She bore six children. Two died shortly after they were born. In 1928, when her last child was born, she returned to work, this time as a dress finisher in the Garment District, which was near their home. During the Depression when she couldn't get work she "took in buttons." Pietro or one of the boys would take the bread wagon to the Garment District and return with a load of cards and buttons. Petrina and whatever children she could collar would sew the buttons on the cards. The pay varied from twenty-five to fifty cents per gross of buttons, and by this means the family could earn ten or more extra dollars each week.

Pietro was as simple as the bread he baked. He worked, saved his money, and made no enemies. His children helped in the bread business as they grew old enough to work, and for years the family lived what has been called "the rich content of the old proletarian city life" in a community made comfortable by the presence of other Italians with similar values. The bread business exacted long hours and co-ordination. In the early days the couple mixed the dough by hand and baked the bread together. Pietro delivered the bread with a pushcart, calling out in his Sicilian dialect, which made the word for bread, *pane*, sound like *ooh-bana*. Eventually the business was big enough to afford a mixing machine and a horse and wagon. By then, the children could help. Angelo and Katie made the dough late at night, let it rise, and shaped the loaves. Willie and Mario built a wood fire in the oven. The ashes were raked off and the bread was baked on the hot bricks, small loaves first, large loaves last. Angelo would wake before daylight and walk to the stables on Thirty-eighth Street to fetch the horse and wagon. By six-thirty in the morning Pietro was ready to start out with his helper, often Mario, who would run the bread into stores and homes. By 1940 "Giaimo and Sons" were baking nearly three hundred loaves a day and delivering them in a panel truck. Their route extended from the Twenties to the Sixties between Ninth and Eleventh Avenues. It was chewy, hard-crusted bread, and the secret of its quality, according to Pietro, was the wood-fired oven, its fuel either delivered by wood dealers or gathered by the youngest son, Mario, who roamed the West Side docks with a claw hammer in his belt.

But Pietro wasn't a man to change his ways too radically. There were gas lines into the tenements, and Mario tried to convince his father to use the gas to fire the oven. This, he argued, would increase productivity. This would enable them to sell more bread, not only to individual customers and small stores, but to bigger stores, to supermarkets. But Pietro said the bread wouldn't cook, that gas wouldn't heat the bricks. Besides that, he had other worries. He and his new son-in-law, Emilio, had just bought a house in Jackson Heights. Both families were now living in Queens; Pietro was keeping the apartment on Thirty-third Street only for the bread business.

The move to Queens made it harder for Pietro to co-ordinate his labor, and as Mario so often reminded him, "You can't steal wood in Queens." With the onset of World War II his oldest sons had also become less enthusiastic about mixing dough and delivering bread. Military pay was more than they could make at home, too. By 1942 Angelo and Willie had both been drafted and this put an end to the bread business. Pietro started working as a laborer at the New York Central Railroad yard on West Seventy-second Street, finding the job through Emilio's father, Vincenzo Panella.

The Giaimo family was a happy one, maybe happier than the Panella family, given to simple philosophizing about work and food, sensitive to slights, frugal but not selfish. America confronted them with a more radical culture change than the Neapolitans encountered, and they met this by clinging to their old ways more tenaciously. They weren't comfortable with Grace's marriage to Emilio, a Neapolitan they weren't comfortable with Mario's marriage to an Irish woman. They prefaced all non-Italian foods with the word "American," and thus we sometimes ate "American" bread, usually Silvercup, or drank "American" coffee, also known as "brown coffee." They had absolutely no interest in politics, although my grandfather did vote when the Democratic Party workers came to his house: he thought they were from the Government. There were very few books in their home, certainly none in Italian. My uncles and grandfather made strong wine every year and stored it in barrels in the cellar. My grandfather drank it from a clay jug brought from Sicily. When the year's supply was finished, he bought the cheapest red wine he could find and drank that with equal enjoyment.

They set their limits in life and moved within them. Yet they were distinct, vivid people. Their influence on my life was stronger than I ever realized, and their repetitions—like Homeric devices—became my burning images. My grandparents kept holy relics in their bedroom, that sanctuary with its cheap alarm clock, a burning candle before the statue of the Virgin Mary in a glass enclosure, a black crucifix, a holy picture of Jesus with a flame burning on top of his heart, the posed studio photographs taken in Italy. Every Monday my grandfather fried potatoes and eggs, ate some for breakfast, and took the rest to work in a sandwich. For breakfast he drank day-old coffee and milk, scalded to a foam. He would wash fresh snails and leave them overnight in pots with weighted covers; the next morning the covers would be slightly lifted and the snails on the march, down the side of the pot and up the kitchen wall. Whenever I found a job, he wouldn't ask what the work was like: he only wanted to know when payday was. He walked the streets of Jackson Heights like an inspector, turning his head from side to side with the frequency of a radar detector, alert for any change in his surroundings. How many times had I watched my grandmother stir a pot of tomato sauce, or gently blow the steam from a boiling pot of macaroni, then set the large, shallow bowl of ziti or rigatoni on the table, saying *ah-boshta* for *pasta*. She burned her Easter palm every year and buried the ashes in the garden. At Easter she also baked wheat pies, and fat cookies curled around hard-boiled eggs. She cleaned ears by rolling a piece of starched linen into a cone, putting the tip

01 West Thirty-third Street, Manhattan

1978

Pietro Giaimo and Petrina Bruno Giaimo

1914

Petrina   1910

Petrina   1948

Pietro and Petrina with a friend   1938

Pietro   Queens, 1977

into a person's ear, and lighting the other end: the flame drew out the wax. In her last years she spoke of dying in terms of joining her brother, Paul, and did more praying than ever, pacing the length of the house with a rosary wrapped around her fingers, moving her lips in a rapid whisper of Sicilian.

The Giaimo children are generally close to their parents in outlook. Angelo, the oldest son, is most conservative, like his father. He tried to curb his younger brothers' vices, but, also like his father, he couldn't. Willie and Mario were close together, drinkers and gamblers. They enjoyed playing on their father's and Angelo's strait-laced outlook, frugality, and sense of wonder. Mario has never forgotten that his father refused to bake the bread with city gas. Today he paints a picture of a multimillion-dollar empire with Giaimo-wrapped Italian bread lining the shelves at Key Food and the A & P. At meals Willie and Mario would tease their father about his stinginess with the homemade wine, and make fun of the way he followed people through the house and shut off the lights behind them. They pretended they were hurt when he signed over his "Italian villa" in Sicily to his brother, Vittorio. Mario once tried to explain the atomic bomb to his father, speaking in his characteristic mixture of Italian and English. Pietro wouldn't believe it until his older sons, Angelo and Willie, affirmed that one bomb—"As big as this kitchen table right here!"—could destroy a city as large as New York. This was a playful kind of interaction; behind it lay the disparity between their generations, the difference in values between Italy and America, and the attempt by Pietro's sons to "explain" America to their father.

The disparity between them was not as wide as they thought. The second generation reveals its Sicilian traces very clearly. Except for a short marriage, Katie has always lived with her father. Angelo lives three blocks away, Willie a mile away in the same neighborhood, Mario sixty miles upstate, and Grace, my mother, a few miles from Mario. And with the exception of myself and one sister—who made our lives in different parts of the country when it suited us—the third generation lives within its family's sphere of influence.

Pietro and Petrina raised their daughters in a traditional Italian way. It was assumed they would marry. Both Katie and my mother quit school at an early age, but this wasn't looked upon with disfavor. After all, there was work to do, for Katie in the bread business, for my mother in the Garment District, first as a pinker, and then as a dress finisher in the same factory as my grandmother. My mother has said that, compared with other parents in the neighborhood, hers weren't strict. In the same breath she remembers Petrina pulling her hair violently and calling her *puttana* when she came home a half hour late. In her case there was probably no reason for apprehension on her parents' part. At sixteen—dating age—she and Emilio were keeping company. Petrina had a mother's affection for the boy. As the youngest of a widower's four children, Emilio was often alone, and there was little to distrust in him. He reciprocated Petrina's affection and free meals by taking out the garbage and doing other chores for her. He was polite, if hotheaded and jealous over Grace. His father was known on the block as a feared disciplinarian, and Emilio was clearly the more level-headed of the two Panella boys. He knew how to save his money. At sixteen he had a car, and a job on the railroad. His eventual marriage to Grace was a foregone conclusion.

My mother, now separated and living alone, remembers those years "like a dream." Teen-age years when life was piano rolls and Guy Lombardo, the dress factory, button sewing, polishing the wood stove in their apartment, and the young man who carried her books to school or turned violently jealous if she spoke to other boys; the young man who forbid her to wear lipstick; the young man who would eventually leave her.

The Giaimo boys were given authority in accordance with age, and the force of the old culture was proportionately transferred. Angelo speaks the best dialect of the three sons, Mario the poorest. When Pietro made his only trip to Italy, in 1929, Angelo was chosen to go. He is a churchgoer, a family man with no vices, and, like his father, reluctant to take chances. After World War II he drove a truck in New York City for five years. He married a Sicilian woman from his old neighborhood; and his final job with the New York City Sanitation Department lasted until his retirement.

Willie is the second oldest and as a boy he took to the streets. In the Tenth Avenue era the railroad cars parked on the streets provided a feast for thieves, and Willie was among them. Stealing was a way of life, and Willie stole ice and coal, commodities readily bought up by the West Side residents. Willie's penchant for theft was matched, if not overmatched, by that curse of the immigrant class—

gambling. His friend, fellow thief, and bosom gambler was the older boy across the street, Frank Panella, my father's brother. Horses were their game, and this habit was fed by proceeds from selling ice, coal, or anything else of value. The war separated the two men temporarily. Willie was a naval gunner on a merchant ship and a translator at Italian ports. During the war he polished up some of his old skills, doing a brisk business in government goods, his specialty being sheets for the Arabs, sheets which he sometimes cut in half and sold as doubles.

After the war he and Frank bought a nine-thousand-dollar trucking business called Smiley's Express, a four-truck outfit delivering anywhere in the metropolitan area, a business bankrolled by my father and Pietro. Smiley's Express employed Mario as a truck driver, and a seven-year-old nephew named Vincent as a part-time helper. But Frank and Willie spent as much time at the Long Island racetracks as they did at work, and by 1947 they'd gambled themselves out of business.

It was the youngest, Mario, who felt most trapped between two cultures. He was a teen-ager when the Giaimo family left the West Side for Queens. There, somewhat like me, he was dropped into the boiling schoolyard culture, into the ethnic mix. He and his friends saw their families as out of fashion, out of reality. They saw America as a money game and they believed the Hollywood dreams. Mario was trouble for his father. He drank, he fought, he gambled, perhaps more recklessly than his brother Willie. He played all the schoolyard sports, but always, it seemed, for money. His outlook became hedonistic. Like all gamblers, he believed in easy money.

In our two-family house in Queens the Giaimo family lived upstairs, the Panella family downstairs, and the basement was common. Here we ate our holiday meals, men played cards, and to the limits of my tolerance and their patience I learned about the old culture. Petrina's cooking reflected not only the richness of Sicily but the Neapolitan influences from their years on the West Side. She sang while she cooked, and no wonder: America had given them money for all the food they wanted. She spent whole weekends making pizza, mixing dough on Saturday and letting it rise between layers of fresh, floury linen. On Sunday she'd bake the thick, square pies, oily on the bottom, tomatoey and heavy with oregano on top, pies generously given out to family and neighbors.

72

Our home was essentially a closed system; America was outside it. The descendants of Pietro and Petrina have paid the price for this unavoidable cultural isolation. The less obvious Sicilian ways had limited use in America. Modest aims, steady work, sexual attitudes characterized by Old World taboos and strict Catholic precepts did poor service to the men, and poorer service to the women: they didn't have the freedom of the streets where they could test the family teachings. The men could see that modest goals led to modest ends, while the streets provided examples of others working less and earning more. The women, like my aunt and mother, unable to counteract America's more permissive sexuality from their posts in the kitchen, became the more damaged victims of failed marriages. Finding themselves without husbands, they were unable to seek new love or new careers. Today they are matrons who nurse their pride with a Mediterranean fatalism, women who bear loneliness with a quiet dignity, but women who are nevertheless alone.

This side of my family still possesses what sociologists might call the "south-Italian village outlook"—this not only means a strong family orientation, but a poor self-image engendered by centuries of exploitation and discrimination in the south of Italy. The resignation to misfortune, the expectation of it, the reluctance to change one's life—this is the village outlook surviving in Queens.

There is truth to the stereotyped Sicilian who characterizes himself as coming from "the place where the gangsters come from," who deprecates his soft-edged, less Germanic and non-textbook dialect, a source of derision for socially tenuous Italians eager to shed prejudice southward. The same man may tell you, with some pride, that the Italian spoken in the film *The Godfather* was "real Sicilian." It was, and the remark is both deprecating and healthy. Deprecating because a Sicilian must identify himself by means of Hollywood's romantic renditions, healthy because part of that rendition is accurate. How many Sicilians, and southern Italians whose dialect is within range of Sicilian, saw *The Godfather* and felt, at last, a sense of pride that their language and lifeways were equally capable of being larger than life, that these qualities were appended to the noble virtues of the Corleone family? With the exception of such opportunities for a public display of identity, Sicilian pride is below the surface. And while there is also the Sicilian who reacts to any stereotype with a fierce pride, the Sicilian who bitterly refuses to even consider himself "Italian," he is not a member of my family. Sicilians, like all Italians, have a distinct provincial culture. And it is common for them and other Italians to joke about the island as being more African than Italian. But there is truth in this line of humor, as a visit to Sicily and a look at its history will testify.

The Sicilians in my family never discussed these matters. But this matter of *Sicilian-ness* is the old, hidden line of force which points to the gap between them and other Italians. It is the original and still existent wedge between my parents. And while being Sicilian is felt to a still lesser degree by the younger generations, the village outlook, for better and worse, has yet to work itself free. In the Giaimo family the Sicilian influence derives from a quietly rigid culture, a culture which has learned to turn its back on the complexities of the outside world while still existing in it. This is village Sicilian, a paradoxical mixture of outward simplicity and self-abasement, consummate frugality, a tendency to think in terms of disaster, strong, subliminal family cohesion, and a rarely discussed pride.

For my family the real immigration came with the move to Queens. This was a more decisive separation from a southern Italian environment than the passage to America. And the Giaimo family moved, not to an Italian section of Queens, but to an Irish and Jewish one. Here there were no neighbors with whom to nurture pride in the old culture while sharing the process of Americanization. The lives of the second-generation Sicilians became characterized by quiet withdrawal: Bingo once a week, the racetrack on occasion, and little or no politics. Other Italians, who would have provided economic opportunities on the West Side, are absent. The family is now a Sicilian island in a changing ethnic current, its original waters now thickened with Spanish-speaking people. It is a neighborhood of sullen streets and locked doors.

The third generation awoke to this environment still influenced by its circumspect Sicilian background. My uncle Mario's maxim—"You can't steal wood in Queens"—applies to them as well. Opportunities commensurate with *their* ability must be sought away from home. But this generation has inherited a great deal of Sicilian caution, and remains close to home. Thus the group is unable to achieve its full potential despite being better educated. This is the danger: that the emigration from Italy will stagnate.

The Giaimo children

Angelo, Mario, and Willie   1944

Grace and Katie   1937

Willie   1945

Grace and Katie with friends   1934

Mario with friends   1943

race   Newburgh, N.Y., 1974

Angelo with Vincent   Queens, 197

Katie   Queens, 197

Willie with his wife, Marie

Queens, 1977

Mario with Vincent

Washingtonville, N.Y., 1977

Love Stories

History placed less of a burden on the Neapolitans: it didn't dampen their expectations. The Panella brothers who came to America were quick to spot an opening, quicker to diverge into riskier paths. The four men were literate, more volatile, willing to challenge authority, and more attached to the old country, where their lives weren't so harsh. They were rural Italians, but their small village was the suburb of a city. Their home was overcrowded, but behind it was a garden large enough to feed the growing family reasonably well. They came here less to survive than to improve themselves and they took root methodically, the oldest brother immigrating before 1900 and building a base for the next brother.

My grandfather, Vincenzo, arrived at age seventeen. Not much is told about his earliest activities, but he is remembered as taciturn and violent, "a man's man" in my uncle Mario's words. Both sides of my family loved and respected him. But he was an unlucky fellow, unlucky in love and life, motivated to make money, but without the compromising and gregarious personality required for success in business. In 1906 he married Consiglia Rubano, an American-born Italian whose hometown was near his own, and according to some, he bragged about the status imparted by her American birth.

At that time in New York City there was a great deal of violence between Irish and Italians: this had much to do with my family's attitude toward the Irish. By 1910, when Vincenzo was operating his tavern, his life on the streets and at work was constantly threatened by the Irish, whether in the form of roving gangs, which were infamous at that time, or by corrupt police. Being a contentious man, he carried a pistol. One day the inevitable occurred. Two policemen entered his bar, accused him of harboring prostitutes, and threatened to close him down unless he gave them money. There was a shooting. Nobody was hurt badly, but Lone Ranger style, Vincenzo had shot the gun from one policeman's hand.

The trouble was smoothed over, but not completely. Through his brother Pasquale—who knew some men of influence—Vincenzo avoided jail and charges. But he had to leave the city. He sold the bar and with his wife and two-year-old daughter, Jenny, moved to a rented farm in Madison, Connecticut, where he and two brothers tried their hand at fruit and chicken raising. Frank and Sylvia were born. A fourth child died. In 1913 he returned to the West Side. The trouble was over, and he began working as a plumber's helper on the New York Central Railroad, a job secured through his brother Pasquale. Vincenzo prepared for a quieter life. Consiglia became pregnant with a fifth child in 1914, but she was exhausted from the ordeal of four children in six years and an unsettled home life. A doctor advised that she have her fifth child in a more tranquil environment than Hell's Kitchen. With her three children she was sent back to Vincenzo's town of Pastene.

An unlucky combination of circumstances prevented Vincenzo from seeing his wife again. Early in 1915 Emilio—my father—was born. But Vincenzo couldn't travel to Italy because World War I had broken out and travel to Italy was forbidden. By 1918, when the travel ban was lifted, Consiglia's life was taken by a worldwide epidemic of Spanish influenza. But now the immigration laws stood between Vincenzo and his family. If he wanted to be naturalized, and he did, he had to remain in America until 1922. Thus he missed Emilio's birth—requesting a nude photograph to verify the child's sex—and he couldn't be with his wife during her last days. He was also prevented from raising his children during their formative years. To my father the man who came to Italy to fetch them in 1922 was a stranger.

In 1922 the Panella children and their widowed father returned to America and took a railroad flat on the top floor at 500 West Thirty-third Street, a tenement adjacent to Pasquale Panella, and across the street from the bread-baking Giaimo family. Vincenzo's daughters were fourteen and eleven years old, his sons nine and seven. With the exception of Jenny, they spoke no English. They had no mother. There was no business in the home, like the bread business, to keep the family together. Pasquale and his wife, Zia Angelina (pronounced "Tingelina"), could exert minimal authority from their nearby apartment when Vincenzo was at work.

His problem was to keep his job and discipline his children, to keep them off the streets and, more important, away from bad influences. The children had never lived with steady authority, even in Italy. Their father wasn't always home, even though he was a feared man and quick to use his hands. The children, or three of them anyway, had to contrive to enjoy their freedom and avoid his discipline. The crowded West Side, with its railroad tracks on the streets, its Neapolitan neighbors, its Irish section north of Thirty-fourth Street, presented the children with the security of an Italian community which could be used as a base for a kind of crime and violence unique to America. For the children the first order of business was to learn to fight those who teased them—usually the Irish. The second was to learn English. Frank and Emilio saw additional horizons. The boys were new to city ways, but they were good learners and quick to take advantage. Flush toilets, for example, frightened the boys at first, then became objects of derision, and a source of fun. And they quickly took up what my father had called "the scavenging life," stealing whatever was salable, mainly ice and coal from the poorly attended railroad cars, or copper and lead from vulnerable buildings. In the coal-burning and prerefrigerator days there was a brisk market for coal and ice, readily brought by fellow Italians. The brothers were soon equipped for theft: strong rope and tongs for fishing blocks of ice through the tops of railroad cars, a wagon for moving the swag, and plumbing tools, some "borrowed" from their father and used to relieve old buildings of their valuable pipe and fixtures.

Vincenzo could control them only when he was home. To Jenny, the oldest, he gave the responsibility for housework and discipline. But a teen-ager, no matter how mature, couldn't counteract the influence of the streets. She also had interests of her own. Before coming back to America she had promised herself to a young man in Pastene, and her first few years in this country were spent with this promise in mind. She kept her father's house and sewed a trousseau for a marriage which would never take place. She was her father's favorite. She was obedient and reliable. She tried to keep

83

Frank and Emilio in line, but he understood this was impossible. Toward Sylvia her feelings were divided. She was loyal to the younger sister brought closer by their mother's death in Italy, but she was also loyal to her father, whose plight she understood, probably more fully than her sister and brothers. At sixteen Jenny went to the Garment District to work. It had become clear by then that the Panella family was in America for good, and she was too. She would never return to Pastene to marry that young man. Household duties were passed on to the younger Sylvia, but this did nothing to improve the state of discipline in Vincenzo's home.

The family again tried to help. Pasquale and Angelina arranged a meeting with a Sicilian woman named Chiarina, who owned a grocery store on Thirtieth Street. Vincenzo made it clear that his interest was based on a desire to have a mother's hand over his children. Chiarina in turn would have the status and companionship of marriage. The courtship wasn't brief, and there was certainly some mutual reluctance and distrust. Chiarina was a cold, hard Sicilian businesswoman, half-owning the grocery store with her brother, and investing in other property on the West Side. She suffered from obesity caused by diabetes, and was surely aware that Vincenzo wasn't primarily motivated by her beauty. She, if not her brother, felt excessive calculation in his interest.

He in turn was worried that Chiarina's interest in the grocery store would remain unchanged by the marriage. He wanted a constant hand over his children. And, being a cynical fellow, he designed his courtship to test her compatibility. He not only called on her with his children in hand, but he often left one or two of his daughters to sleep with her in the small apartment behind the store. He was hoping that her strict attitudes, and the grocery store itself, would provide an atmosphere of restraint. He arranged it so Chiarina's most frequent overnight guest was his highest risk, Sylvia. Unlike Jenny, Sylvia had no early interest in marriage. She was a physically mature, black-haired beauty in the Mediterranean style, romantic, given to dangerous flights of the imagination, and increasingly rebellious as her father sought to restrain her movement. She didn't like America very much either, not at first anyway. She was sensitive to teasing at school because of her broken English, and she had constant fistfights, especially with non-Italian girls. She often made her father walk her to the Hudson River; there she would ask why they couldn't go back over the ocean to Italy. But at other times, even under his scrutinizing and suspicious eye, she was cunningly flirtatious. Vincenzo knew she was capable of disobedience. But he couldn't watch her all day, and he couldn't give her the female understanding she needed.

Chiarina wasn't the candidate for the job either. Instead of providing Sylvia with motherly discipline, she became the unwitting instrument of the young girl's freedom. While sleeping with Chiarina behind the store Sylvia discovered that the woman kept her store receipts in a small cloth bag tucked between her breasts. Each day Chiarina parted company with the bag just once: when she took her morning bath. Sylvia soon discovered that the bag was tied too tightly to open quickly, but by manipulating the bills with her fingers she could squeeze them out one at a time. She did this for two years, rising to thievery while Chiarina took her bath, and pretending to be asleep when the woman returned to the bedroom. Chiarina never discovered the loss; but Frank and Emilio did, and their price for silence was a share of the money. The boys were living by their wits then. They shunned the poorly paying jobs open to boys their age. By 1931, when he was sixteen, my father was taking taxicabs to school (which he quit that year) or driving around the neighborhood in his 1918 Packard touring car.

Shortly before the marriage of Chiarina and Vincenzo, Sylvia ran away from home. Her father's restrictions had become unbearable. With the few hundred dollars saved from Chiarina's money she rented a furnished room and began a thirteen-year exile from her father, brother, and sisters, a period of her life which she never discussed. Feeling that he'd been dishonored before his neighbors, Vincenzo swore to kill her on sight. Those who knew him believed him. But he went ahead with his marriage even though the major reasons for it were no longer valid: Sylvia had run away; Jenny had married; Frank and Emilio, seventeen and thirteen years old at the time, were too wild to fall under Chiarina's halfhearted attempts at control. She was, as my father said, "a cash register woman," unable to generate emotion for family life.

Vincenzo was a brooding, serious man who wanted more wealth than a job on the railroad would give him. With his extra money he bought and sold penny stocks, and at one point tried to work in the grocery store. But he couldn't deal with the public. He wasn't genial.

Vincenzo Panella

Vincenzo with Consiglia, Sylvia, Jenny, and Frank   1914

Vincenzo with Chiarina   1929

On the railroad   Manhattan, 1925

Vincenzo with his brother, Giuseppe   Queens, 1942

Queens, 1943

He took offense too easily. His railroad job was more suitable. In the uptown yard he'd become foreman of the steam-fitting shop. Here he could be a taskmaster on familiar ground, ordering men to perform clearly defined tasks.

Over the years Vincenzo became a sullen, violent drinker, often unleashing his anger at home. He felt betrayed on two sides, by his wife, by his daughter. He had little home life. Jenny was married and living in the Bronx. Frank had set himself in life as a gambler. Emilio was more responsible, but young and distant. Both boys had married Sicilians. In 1940, after a drinking spree in which he wrecked his apartment, he had a stroke. Jenny came to Manhattan and took him to her apartment. Chiarina moved back to the grocery store. The marriage was finished. She died of a stroke that year.

He and Sylvia made up in 1941. She'd been waiting for his anger to subside, and by then was keeping in touch with her sister and brothers. Learning of his stroke and subsequent sickness, she wondered if he would reconcile with her. She'd left New York by then, changed her name, and taken a factory job in New Jersey. There she'd met and married a well-mannered engineer named Albert J. D'Ambrosio. With her image enhanced by marriage to a professional man, and a Neapolitan, she sounded Jenny out: would her father see her? Jenny set up a meeting at her apartment. Sylvia drove there with Albert and went into the apartment alone. She saw him sitting with his back to her. When he turned to face her, she saw how much he'd aged. He looked her up and down, slowly, then got up and left the room.

"I knew he wasn't ready," she said to Jenny.

Jenny told her to wait. She joined her father in the next room and spoke to him. Then she brought him back. Sylvia saw it would be all right. They embraced. Albert was called up from the car; he made a fine impression on his father-in-law.

Vincenzo aged very quickly after his stroke. He lived with Jenny for less than a year, but it wasn't the place to recuperate. She had three mischievous boys who teased the old man, sometimes cruelly: they made fun of his broken English, threw his straw hat on the trolley tracks, and once blew pepper in his face while he lay sick in bed. He came to our house in Queens. Life was more peaceful with his old neighbors, Pietro and Petrina. Vincenzo (by then called Jimmy) and Pietro (now Pete) played *briscola* at night and went to work together during the day. How often, hungry for supper and knowing I wouldn't eat until they came home, did I wait for them on the corner of Seventy-sixth Street and Thirty-seventh Road. I'd watch them turn the corner and come toward me as steady as time, Pete short and thick, Jimmy tall and gaunt.

He didn't speak much and I didn't like to kiss him because his moustache bruised my lips. But he ordered me to kiss him, he never asked, and I always complied. He slept in his own room and lived with us for two years. In 1944 he died of a stroke and they buried him at Calvary Cemetary on Queens Boulevard. My parents emptied his room of all his belongings and decorated it with new wallpaper: fox hunters with hounds and horses. The room was given to me. I was five years old when he died and his was my first funeral. Mostly I remember Sylvia, crying hard, a black veil covering her face. There was quite a bit of screaming and knuckle biting, the emotional display which I came to dread. A few years later I went to a second funeral at the same funeral parlor in Jackson Heights. Jenny's husband, Tony, had committed suicide.

Tony Quaglietta had been my father's partner in a number of uptown bars. I mention his death—he was a generous man and a very heavy gambler—to show the bad luck and irregular terrain crossed by the Neapolitan side of the family. They lived faster, they died younger: my grandfather at sixty-one, Frank at forty-eight, Jenny at sixty-eight, Sylvia at sixty-seven. None had a stable married life. Frank was divorced from his first wife; he lived out of wedlock with the woman who became his second. My father separated twice from my mother, the last time apparently for good. He has been living with another woman for several years but they aren't married. Sylvia's marriage to Albert was interrupted by a long separation: he died shortly after they were reconciled. Jenny never remarried, but she and Sylvia were resilient enough to do what the Sicilian women in my family couldn't do: they had male friends and they went to work. Jenny and Sylvia started a small women's clothing store. Jenny also bought a decaying day school in Jamaica and turned it into a profitable business. She was a sleepless, restless woman who fell asleep to the muted, late-night television, coffee and cigarettes in front of her. My grandmother often said that Jenny was born with a tail because she could work like a man. She died of a stroke in 1976, while I was in Italy.

The Panella children

Arrival in America   1922

Emilio Panella   1915   Jenny with Tony   1929

Sylvia   1939

Emilio and Frank   1941

Jenny and Sylvia   1948

Sylvia with Al, Frank with Jean   1942

Sylvia

Newburgh, N.Y., 1977

Grandpa and Sylvia

"I want to be a singer when I grow up."
"You can be a singer, but it must be opera."
"I'll be a nurse, then."
"No."
"Why not?"
"As a nurse you will see men."
"I'll be a nurse anyway."
"You can be a midwife, not a nurse."

Italy

Before going south I spent some time in the popular part, Venice, Florence, Rome, traveling by train, wanting to go to Naples and Sicily but delaying it, apprehensive because I had no idea what to expect. The longer I toured in the north, the more apprehensive I became. I was hovering over southern Italy, preoccupied with my visits there as I tried to take in the famous art I'd known only from books. Something was going to happen down there but I didn't know what it was, some climax, some crisis, or more likely some comic and inconclusive finish to my presumption that in fact there was family in Italy which considered itself connected to me.

I had to go through with those visits if only because the preparations had been elaborate—college courses in Italian grammar and conversation where the condescending instructors tried to repair my built-in dialect tendencies, and photographs and letters sent to the Giaimo and Panella families in Italy.

It was easy to see why people loved Italy without reservation. It didn't have the discipline of France, nor the dry, barren solitude of Spain. But one can't be blind to the politics, the inflation, the unemployment, the confusion. Otherwise Italy is what they say it is: flowers, fruits, and fresh vegetables everywhere, luscious food, visual sensuality, friendly people, and the language like background music. But Italy's trouble can't be shunted aside today, certainly not by the tourist. The government doesn't work, and this makes everything uncertain, from the price of a cup of coffee and whether one can buy it, to the arrival time of a train.

I entered Italy from France by train and the line of demarcation between the two countries was distinct. The first sight of the country was a half-ruined city with abandoned and vandalized buildings, wandering chickens and goats, and those ubiquitous block-shaped homes with mortar crumbling between the stones. And yet the laundry rigged between the houses swung slowly in the clear sunlight, crowning the streets with a brightness which forgave the general drabness and neglect.

In the countryside all the tillable land was utilized, the flatland planted with rice, wheat, and vegetables, the hills sloping to the Apennines dense with grapevines, flowering fruit, and budding olive trees. Hand-shaped leaves hung from the vines, and edibles sprouted everywhere: artichokes, apricots, broccoli, beans, tomatoes, cherries, and varieties of fruits and vegetables I couldn't identify. Larger, more ornate homes were set higher up in the wooded hills, or perched on rocky promontories, houses faced with colored stucco, yellow faded to oyster, red gone to pink or sienna. The tinier villages near the railroad tracks were clusters of square houses, each with a small garden and a chicken coop.

In Rome the letters and telegrams with news of Jenny's death caught up. As the train to Naples shot through the tunnels and clacked violently over the flats, I felt the old hold of family guilt. I'd neither seen nor made an effort to visit my aunt in at least ten years. Sylvia was alive then. I knew she took this death hard. She explained in her letter that she'd lost not only a sister but a close friend and mother. True to his fashion, my father went about his business right after the funeral. He was hiding his grief and it would tumble out later. Approaching Naples, I carried her presence with me. Like my grandmother Petrina, she was an archetypal woman, one who could exercise great powers while seeming to succumb to a man, a woman constantly on the move and working for her family. Because of her special relationship with her father she had the strongest sense of family of all the Panella children. To her own children she imparted the family lore, the stories of generations past in Italy. Her death put a mournful nostalgia on my trip at exactly the point when I was ready to visit the town where she had matured, and where my father was born.

The train compartment was shared with a burly Calabrian and a young, unshaven Neapolitan. The subject was politics. The Calabrian was a carpenter and a Communist, a dark fellow with a glossy and voluminous moustache, and a straight party line: the government must be purged from top to toe. He used the word "gangster" continually. Gangsters were everywhere. Gangsters were hoarding coins so Italians couldn't make the simplest purchase. Gangsters with access to tax records were kidnaping the wealthy and hiding them in the hills while the police looked the other way. President Leone was a gangster because he made three salaries: one as President, one as a law professor whose subordinates did the teaching, and another as a lawyer whose clients were also gangsters.

The Neapolitan looked to heaven and clasped his hands in a sign of futile impatience with this fellow. He'd already explained in halting English that he was a college graduate who'd been unemployed for two years. In his wrinkled and poor quality clothes he looked like a caricature of the wealthy Italian male: soiled shirt unbuttoned to the chest, cluster of charms and medals quite visible, the overnight bag at his feet made of poor quality vinyl. He finally engaged the Calabrian. In moments the arguments were fast and furious. My Italian wasn't good enough for me to join in. I wondered what they thought of me, an American in Levis and sturdy boots touring their country and buying intangibles. But for a decision or two I would have been that Neapolitan with the drum-tight stomach and the cluster of charms around his neck. He and the Calabrian were intractable in their arguments. Neither listened to the other. The younger man clearly considered him to be a dogmatic simpleton.

When the train slowed for Naples they wished me well and issued the warnings I would soon be familiar with: a finger placed under the eye to signify that I must be *furbo*, watchful, and guard against *i ladri*, the thieves, who swoop down on Vespas or lean out of passing cars to snatch shoulderbags.

The city was noisy, dirty, and fast. The horde of taxi drivers in front of the train station had no system for the first fare. A traveler is buttonholed by a group of eager men, each trying to conceal his price and not lose the fare. On the street I saw a woman throttle a little boy because he was crying too much. He continued crying. She shook his shoulders again. He burst out once more. She slapped his face. He bit his lip to hold back the tears. Some women walking past commented on the scene, talking out of the sides of their mouths the way my Aunt Jenny used to talk: "Go get me a quart of milk," she'd say, slipping me the money, the degree of conspiracy out of all proportion to the event. In Naples people gave directions with the same secret intimacy, as if together we were allied against a hostile world.

There were few police on the streets, which were congested with noisy and uncontrolled traffic. Taxicabs drove against the oncoming traffic, then cut back into their lanes at the last possible moment. Idle men were everywhere, most of them young, on corners, in cafes buying nothing, at bus and train stations looking for possibilities. Here I saw the great Italian weaknesses: intelligence impeded by ego, ambition restricted by inflation and unemployment. Inflation there was more palpable than in America. Increased labor only results in less buying power. This produces a frustration, a violence toward one's surroundings. A man throws a half-eaten apple onto the train track when a litter basket is in sight. Men punish their cars for being small. People hoard coins because they don't trust paper money. In the shortage of coins which still exists in Italy every purchase is a contest of will between a store owner wanting exact change and a customer wanting more change so he can make his next purchase with less aggravation. You may ride the bus free by showing the conductor a bill he cannot change: a five-thousand-lire note will do.

At first, I was puzzled by the southern Italian attitude toward history. I walked through the Pompeii *scavi* with a feeling of wonderment so strong I could have been a rube from *The Innocents Abroad*. How easy to extrapolate to the past. In the city forum three attendants sat in the shade, smoking, not talking, sitting there like three old pieces of leather in their attitudes of boredom, disinterest, perhaps hostility. They were tired of selling their history.

Italy suffers from a crisis in pace. People move fast but don't get far. In Paris there's a well-timed elegance to the service in the most crowded cafe. But in Italy, and especially in the south, you may be the only person in a cafe at the slowest time of day, and if he can make change, the young man behind the counter will produce a cup of coffee with a crashing fury of chrome and china. "Look how fast I am!" he is saying. Yet when the cafe gets crowded there is confusion. *Padroni* don't trust their help, so the procedure for a purchase is to pay for a chit in a booth and present it at the counter. This doesn't encourage a second purchase.

Naples, 1976

My Roots

"I am Vincent Panella, from America."

Thus my visit began, with a phone call from a cafe and a pre-rehearsed sentence. For hours I'd walked the wide, nearly empty streets in the factory district of Benevento. I examined the sweets and *liquori* in the downtown shops, the mass-produced goods in the UPIM department store. I perused the city's main tourist attraction, Trajan's Arch, a monument to the Appian Way. I was killing time, debating whether to get back on the train and go to Sicily first. But there I'd also get cold feet at the prospect of visiting relatives whose hospitality was uncertain.

I thought of abandoning both visits. So what if I saw the towns and houses where they were born? Why was I risking rejection by relatives I knew so little about? How many Americans had done this? I thought about my embarrassment when friends asked if I was going to Italy to "find my roots." My roots! Any person in the streets of Benevento could have introduced himself to me as a Panella and I would have believed it. Earlier that afternoon I'd taken the train from Naples which climbed slowly up and over the mountains. It was hot in the crowded coach. People were sweaty and irritable. They looked like a random sample of Italy—commuters in suits and ties, older women in black, younger women in tight jeans. I imagined embarrassing scenes in which various people in the coach would turn out to be my relatives.

We look for something visceral in these places, some anchor to hold us steady on the earth. Those without such a place create one. Those with one embellish it. I saw my father's family through the filter of this ordinary-looking part of Italy, a small city damaged by air raids in World War II, a city with its measure of antiquity: a major junction on the road from Rome to Brindisium, a base for Roman conquest of the south, the site of several battles for control of the south, ruled by Ostrogoths and Lombards, owned by the papacy, then by the French. Thus my anchor slides back into history.

What could I gain or learn by *physically being* in the place where they were born unless by some gloss of the imagination? And what if with a cold Neapolitan sense of reality, my father's cousin Mario Panella and his family would be put off, or even amused by my presumption of a connection to them? Tenth Avenue was long ago, I told myself. Tenth Avenue wasn't even mine to share. And then there was Jenny's death. What could I offer a grieving cousin? I hadn't seen Jenny in ten years. Would they see that as a lack of respect? During those years I'd been away from home, and Mario had been to America as Jenny's guest. Maybe he considered himself more of a Panella than I. Surely his impression of me had already been formed by my aunts and father, that side of the family least sympathetic to my way of life.

Italian telephones don't inspire confidence in technology, only in loud talking. Reception is poor, and to make a call one must buy a token, dial the number, then insert the token before the answering party hangs up in frustration. The Italian phone greeting is, appropriately, *Pronto! Pronto!*

"*Pronto! Pronto! Sono Vincenzo Panella, dall'America!*"

In loud but far-off Italian: "Vincent! I've been waiting for you!"

One of my roots: cynicism.

Mario looked like a Panella: wide nose, short trunk, and long legs. He came into the cafe with a quick, serious confidence, at once the protector. When he kissed and embraced me with an immediate intimacy, I realized how wrong I'd been to assume the worst. We drove off in his small Fiat, the back seat filled with groceries, and at the first stoplight (where he turned off his motor) he asked if I'd heard any news from home. He spoke with the familiar sauce of Neapolitan intrigue. This was a test of sorts. I recited the other sentence I'd been practicing:

"*Ho ricevuto una lettera dicendo che sua cugina è morta.*"

It sounded so wooden. He didn't reply, but he clearly understood.

As we drove on I told him what I knew: a stroke, several days in the hospital, then death. I offered the few details which Sylvia had supplied me.

With tears in his eyes he began talking about Jenny, using her Italian name, Giannina. He'd seen the way she lived when he visited her in America: the late hours, the coffee and cigarettes, the physical work she put upon herself. He spoke with a sad, subdued anger, a mood abruptly cut short as he told me, carefully, and with slow repetition, that his son and daughter hadn't been told of their aunt's death. They'd become attached to Jenny during her visits to Italy. Now they were medical students, studying in Naples and taking year-end examinations. They would be home for my visit. Mario wanted to wait until their tests were over before he told them. I agreed to the secret. I was not unfamiliar with such secrets. Thus Jenny's death had joined me to Mario in a way that nothing else could.

The Panella family   Pastene, 1955

Pastene, 1976

My Father's Side

The city of Benevento lies in a broad valley and at the confluence of two rivers. A ring of wooded mountains protects it. The valley and surrounding hills are fertile, either dense with foliage and wild flowers or intensely farmed. Crops grow on ground so steep and irregular that a good rain would seem to wash everything away. Yet these tilted patches of loamy earth easily support vines, olive trees, fruits, vegetables, and a good deal of tobacco. There are few mechanized farms. Most of the land is divided into small plots, and these are worked by hand, or with mules.

Pastene, my father's town, is eight kilometers from Benevento on the down side of a southerly foothill. It has one street (paved since my father's day), one church, and a cafe without a sign. Most of the homes are faced with tinted stucco, and their architecture varies. Concrete walls or iron fences separate the bigger houses from the street. It's a hill town, beautiful enough to be called idyllic, but its solitude is too often violated by the snarling car, truck, or motorbike which sends pedestrians scurrying roadside with cries of *"Attenta la macchina!"* In those hills the variety and aroma of wild flowers are overwhelming. The road through the town rises sharply into hills where even smaller towns sit like landings in a spiral staircase. A short walk brings one high enough to see Pastene's single street, the row of houses on either side of it, the sun-bleached church, and the ring of mountains which once protected Benevento from hostile armies.

The Panella house, near the church, is a broad-faced affair with front and rear gardens and a wrought iron fence on the street side.

Mario extended the house in 1960. It had been a five-room home with a wood oven and no running water. Now it is a duplex. Four rooms make up the old apartment now. Mario's family has six. These are sparely furnished and there are few appliances: a small refrigerator, a washing machine, and a small electric water heater which is usually switched off. It is one of the better homes in Pastene, its flower garden well tended, its vegetable garden productive and neatly weeded, large enough to afford the worker who tills it for a share of the crop.

In his teens and early twenties Mario was a long-distance runner who competed nationally. Then he took a government job as a draftsman in a military weapons office. Like an American civil service job, it meant financial security. In Italy it also meant discounts on state-supplied services such as railroads and schools.

To save gasoline, Mario not only turns off his car motor at every stoplight; he also coasts down any hill worth his while. The last few kilometers from Benevento to Pastene are downhill. This he always coasted, crossing himself when he passed the cemetery, and braking through the town so he could turn into his driveway at a safe speed. When he drove me to Pastene for the first time, he interrupted this habitual coast and stopped at the church. We got out of the car and he pointed to the clock in the bell tower. It was ready to strike for the half hour. He pointed out two brass bells and two hammers mounted above the clock face. When the minute hand touched the six, a hammer attached to a rope struck the smaller bell twice. The sound was a delicate "Ting! Ting!" An old family story began taking shape in my mind.

"Do you know this clock?" Mario asked.

"I think so."

"What do you know?"

"It's my grandfather's clock," I said, forcing a memory that Grandpa Panella had something to do with a clock in Italy.

"He put up that clock in 1922, the year he came to bring his children back to America."

How little the clock had meant when I couldn't visualize it, when I didn't know the tradition of churches, clocks, and bell towers in Italy, and when I couldn't relate the clock to an important event in my grandfather's life: his final departure from Italy. Just two weeks before visiting Pastene I'd stood in Venice's Piazza San Marco and watched the crowd cheer a more ornate version of the same clock.

112

So this was the mark of my grandfather, dubbed by Mario "*il uomo serio*," the serious man.

The clock must have been five feet in diameter and forty feet from the ground. A deeper toned bell rang on the hour, its mate on the quarter hour. Mario didn't know how it had been raised into the tower. In 1922 he and my father were seven years old when that strange uncle, and father, returned to collect his children. Why did he buy and install the clock? Not only for his mother, who prayed at that church every day and who'd raised his children; but probably to leave his mark in the town which tempted him to stay. He knew he couldn't remain there, even if the garden was a big one. He had a steady job on the New York Central (plumbing shop foreman to be). There were possibilities that might open up for him, his brothers, his children. The clock was his proper symbol. Let the town forget his mother, forget his wife, even forget him; but let them measure their days with his gift.

Mario was a fast, emphatic speaker whose Italian easily outran my own. He was a reservoir of jokes and stories—most would lose in translation—and well versed in our family's history. He understood what the visit meant to me, and he spent a great deal of time showing me what Pastene was like. Maybe it was Jenny's death, and maybe not, but I sensed in him a feeling that his life was essentially lonely because he was cut off from the four cousins who'd grown up with him, and who'd left in 1922. He said he especially missed my father, who'd never returned to Italy. When talking about him Mario rubs his index fingers together as if trying to produce sparks, and says, "Me and Emilio were like *that*."

I was treated as Mario would treat my father. My plate held the biggest portions of food. I slept in the master bedroom: Mario and Esterina slept on the living-room floor and would hear no protest. One day after my arrival Esterina washed my laundry and hung it out to dry. But I was never alone. If I left the house with hopes of walking by myself, someone always tagged along, if not Mario or Esterina (who loved introducing me to neighbors), then their daughter Vittoria or their son Enrico. The children are in their early twenties and, somewhat like myself, have been raised by a domineering father whose good intentions result in sheltering. A naïve self-consciousness walks beside Vittoria's vehement Communist sentiments, and with Enrico's more traditional male obsessions as well: soccer, rock music, and women.

113

Since Mario couldn't express his sorrow over Jenny's death unless we were alone, he spoke quite a bit about Frank Panella, his cousin and my uncle, the first of Vincenzo's children to pass away. Like my family in America, Mario speaks of him with awe. Frank was handsome, tough, and good-natured, but unlucky at cards and horses. Because he did so poorly in private business, he stayed with the New York City Fire Department. One summer day while turning off a fire hydrant in a poor neighborhood, someone threw a garbage pail which struck him in the head. He received a concussion and was never the same after it. I remember him lifting me over his head when I was sixteen. My mother said he was the toughest kid on Thirty-third Street ("He had some right!"). Unlike my father, he took me fishing. He took my cousins hunting. After Jenny's husband died, Frank served as a father to her children. He was absolutely addicted to horse playing. Once when he was behind on his bills my father lent him money: he took it to the racetrack. He abused cars, he attacked physical work without asking for help. He died of a heart attack at forty-eight, moving a heavy piece of furniture by himself.

Mario knew all these stories. He spoke about his generation with intense feeling and surprising knowledge of their lives considering how little contact there'd been. Behind his talk was the sense of family history, manifested more on the Panella side, the idea that psychological traits were handed down through generations. I knew he'd been looking at me on those terms, trying to fit me into the patterns—which part Sicilian, which part Panella, and, of that part, who I resembled most.

I listened to Mario talk, running after his rapid Italian, forcing him to stop and repeat when I couldn't understand something. He was a well of family history—Queens, Brooklyn, Tenth Avenue—he knew more than I did. He told the story of the shooting in my grandfather's bar. He gave tantalizing and incomplete details of his father Enrico's brief stay in America. He said he was the same age as my father and that as boys they'd shared the same bed. He talked about the way my father withheld his emotions. He spoke about Jenny and Sylvia, how they traveled *prima classe, sempre*, how he took Jenny to Venice where she bought a Murano glass chandelier for her school in Jamaica. I watched him move from humor to tears and back to humor very quickly: he had none of the emotional reticence I'd always associated with the Panella family.

Pastene, 1976

Antonella Carosella

The Church Clock

View from the bell tower

Vittoria Panella

Enrico in front of the Panella home

Esterina Panella

Mario Panella

La Qualità

In Pastene food is the measure of living, not only in the eating, but in the activity which precedes it. Dining is a protracted event. In the morning Mario and Esterina announce the menu and show off the uncooked meats and vegetables, the cheeses, fruits, and salami we will eat that day. They continually use the word *qualità* to show they have bought or grown the best. I never saw Mario or Enrico in the kitchen. The men wait outside and drink an *aperitivo* while Esterina kicks up a frying and clattering fury. Our main meals consist of several courses with small portions, served in the European sequence: pasta first, salad last.

I expected their hospitality to include big meals, but hadn't figured on Esterina's cooking. There is no way to do justice to the freshness and flavor of everything set on the table, and set with an air of confidence, almost arrogance, letting me know that what she cooked was the absolute best. It would be hard to argue with her. She served pasta with a plain tomato sauce which seemed to have nothing in it but fresh tomatoes, a sauce so subtle that other tomato sauces seem crudely polluted with spices. Typical vegetable dish: fresh peas and baby artichokes, steamed, then sautéed in olive oil, served with fresh lemon; or peppers, roasted, peeled, then mixed with garlic, oregano, oil, and chopped anchovy. Meat was usually veal, thinly sliced, fried in oil and lemon. Meals tapered off into green salad, provolone, salami, fresh fava beans eaten from the pod—these were followed by fruits in season. Mario makes his own wine, a dark, clear red, closer to claret than Burgundy. At meals my glass and plate were kept full. I ate seconds. I ate thirds. When I tried to stop Mario from heaping food on my plate, he would say, "*Coraggio!*"—courage—and continue feeding me.

It is a strong experience to travel thousands of miles to a strange country and to find family that takes you in, suddenly and, completely. It was also emotionally tiring, even physically tiring when the language gap forced me to concentrate very hard on what Mario was saying. We did quite a bit of walking, through Pastene, through Benevento. And Mario kept talking. I was getting more than the tour. I was getting what my father would get if he went there—a sharing of lives.

The large garden behind the house has fed the Panella family for generations, and Mario is proud of that. One day as we walked through the rows, and among vines and fruit and nut trees, Mario told me that he'd never wanted to go to America. He blended this conversation with one-word introductions to the produce in his garden. "*Fava!*" he said, ripping a few long green pods from their stalks and snapping them open for me, repeating the word *fava* as if teaching a baby a new word. At a cherry tree he said "*Ciliegia!*" and pulled off a branch end full of red and yellow San Giovanni cherries. "*Ciliegia! Buona!*" he said again, stretching the *uo* double vowel so that the word sounded like "*Bwoona!*" He told me about his draftsman's job in Benevento: like government jobs in America, it wasn't demanding. He would get a pension. He and his family rode the trains at a discount. Yes, Italy had inflation. Meat and gasoline were high. The lira bought less and less. But with his garden, with his peace and security, he'd never had a desire to move. Neither did his children. They hoped to work in the big hospital in Benevento. He'd been to America. He'd seen Jenny's school, Sylvia's big car (a Ford). He'd seen how they lived: big cars, big money, but big misery. He would stay in Pastene, where he was the keeper of the clock. He showed me some tiny walnut and olive trees being nursed along. Some, he said, would be producing when I came to Italy for a second time. He showed me small bunches of grapes already on the vines. He looked at me and said, "Why should we live in America?"

Later he and his family would visit me in Sicily. After arriving they would hold up the food brought from home. Again they would point to its quality. They would assure me of enough food to eat. Mario would scour the markets and stores for the tastiest olives, the freshest fish, the best pasta and olive oil. In the tiny apartment which I'd rented Esterina would cook our meals.

They were fussy about food, finicky beyond their income level. When I cooked them a dinner of roast chicken and tossed salad, they were polite but unexcited. Chicken is a cheaper meat: it lacks the status of veal. I seasoned the salad with ground black pepper and Vittoria thought it was dirt. She wouldn't eat it. During their visit Esterina politely refused to cook with my olive oil. She bought another brand and said it was better. I couldn't taste the difference. Mario claimed Sicilian olives were bigger and tastier than those further north: he was right. He also said that Sicilian table salt was superior, and he took six kilograms of it back to Pastene.

This attitude toward food took root quite easily in America, where Italians could afford to indulge themselves. I saw it at home. The consistent custom of an Italian family is to feed its guests and overfeed itself. *"Mangia! Mangia!"* is an Italian joke with its measure of truth. A scarcity of food produces an obsession with eating. In America this obsession could be satisfied. But in Italy the traditionally poor and inflated economy is a natural curb to overeating. And while the spare life didn't affect the richness and creativity of Italian cooking, it did limit the quantity served at mealtime. Italian butchers slice fresh meat very finely. At the table all portions are small. One doesn't see many overweight Italians.

Patterns

Mario Panella made his only trip to America when I was living in Iowa. But even though we'd never met, I knew about his visit. Aunt Jenny had given him the trip as a gift. He'd gone to her son's wedding. He'd met my sisters. He'd been briefly reunited with my father. Aunt Sylvia had driven him to my mother's house, apparently as a way of showing him family property. They parked outside and didn't go in. My mother had seen them from the window.

One day I asked, "Before you met me, what did you know about me?"

He looked me straight in the eye, made a tremulous gesture with his hand to indicate that his statement wasn't quite what he believed, and said, "That you were a 'playboy.' "

He said "playboy" in English.

We were in Sicily then. The circumstances of his visit had given me the chance to gauge his perception of me. The general delivery letter announcing his visit had reached me late in the afternoon on the day of his arrival. Since I couldn't meet him at the train station, he had to find me without the help of an address. A taxi driver had led him to the tourist complex where I was staying, and my landlord—a man who understood family relationships—described me to Mario as "*un uomo serio,*" a serious man.

Un uomo serio became a humorous catch phrase for the week of Mario's visit, not only because it altered a prior impression which, I was certain, had been supplied by my family, but because Mario had used the phrase to describe my grandfather and my father. Now that he knew me and was trying to establish the lines of my identity,

Mario had been given some independent evidence. I was certain he valued this timely description, and I was glad of it. One reason for my apprehension about visiting relatives in Italy was the obligatory explanation of how I made my living. At the time of my visit to Italy I was teaching part-time, and writing the rest of the time. From my family's point of view I was giving a poor performance in life. Part-time teaching meant part-time money; and writing signified to them a dreamy, lazy life, looking out the window and tapping a typewriter with two fingers. In his more understanding moods my father termed writing "a long shot" and left off the subject. "Playboy" probably made a great deal of sense to Mario at the time of his trip to America. I was in Iowa, and out of touch with my family. Until my landlord's unsolicited opinion and my short stay in Pastene, Mario's only sources of information had been my father and his sisters, a united front in almost all family matters.

I had invited Mario to visit me in Sicily in a thank-you note after my stay at his home. I never thought the invitation would be taken up. In the first place I was uncertain about how closely Mario wanted to hold me. Secondly I knew the trip would be expensive, whether taken by car or train. One afternoon I simply found Mario, Esterina, Vittoria, and Enrico sitting on my terrace, travel weary and frustrated from a seventeen-hour train ride, and puzzled because their letter hadn't reached me in time. Their visit put the seal of intimacy on our relationship. We were more than distant cousins. For a week we shared my small apartment in Cefalù, a fishing and tourist town on Sicily's Tyrrhenian coast. During that time we ate, shopped, swam, and cooked together, the crowded quarters and close living improving my Italian to the point where I didn't need to repeat, refine, or use the dictionary when I wanted to say something.

Mario knew that my trip to Sicily was as important to me as my visit to Pastene. Cefalù was two hours from the town in the mountains where my Sicilian grandparents were born. I'd already been there several times. Mario was sensitive to my loyalties toward my mother's family, and asked me a few cautious and innocuous questions about them. It was clear that because of my parents' separation a meeting between the two families, which might have taken place in Cefalù by coincidence, would have been uncomfortable for both sides.

I learned more about the Panella family's attitude toward Sicilians by watching them interact with the people of Cefalù. They'd never been to Sicily before, but the Panellas looked upon the local people as poor relatives of Italians. They found the dialect a source of gentle humor, the poverty a source of sympathy. Since they hadn't seen enough of the island to realize that the French had left behind their share of blond and red-haired genes (they had left them in Pastene, too), they regarded black hair and dark skin as ubiquitous Sicilian characteristics. *"Che bellezza Sicilia!"* they'd say wistfully, looking off into the castle-like mountains and understanding what an impoverished way of life they held.

Grandpa Giaimo: 1887–1978

This was the measure of his days. He sat at the window and watched the street, the single tree, the patch of garden, the two garbage pails his son Angelo would take in later. Below him people walked briskly to the subway, their heels clacking on the sidewalk. A half block away an el-train passed and vibrated the house slightly.

"I'm going to visit your town, Grandpa."

"What town?"

"Your town in Italy."

"Why you wanna' do that?"

"To see where you and Grandma were born."

He laughed and said, "There's nothing there!"

Later he gave me some things for his brother: twenty dollars, reading glasses, and a pair of galoshes because it snows in his part of Sicily.

His last words were, "Watch out for thieves."

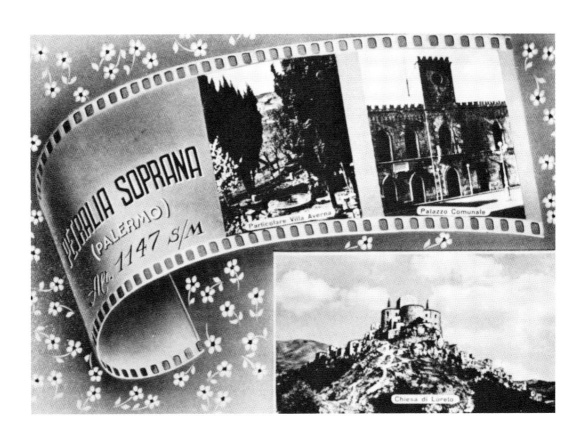

PETRALIA SOPRANA
(PALERMO)
Alt. 1147 S/M

Particolare Villa Averna

Palazzo Comunale

Chiesa di Loreto

Petralia Soprana

When my grandmother pronounced the name of her town she softened the *p*'s, rolled the *r*'s, and stressed the next-to-last syllable of each word. The name would come at me like a rickety cart. As the words *Petralia Soprana* suggest, the village lies on the top of a high, rocky mountain. Most maps of Sicily don't show it. It lies about one hundred kilometers southeast of Palermo, and is said to be the highest village in the Madonie Mountains, a range extending across northeastern Sicily. Sicilians familiar with the town call it Petralia, or simply Soprana. They always distinguish it from Petralia *Sottana*, a sister town, larger, a few kilometers lower on the same mountain.

Both of my Sicilian grandparents came from Petralia, and more relatives lived there than in Pastene. My grandfather's brother, Vittorio Giaimo, had inherited the family home. His three children and their families still lived in Petralia. On my grandmother's side there was a childless and widowed sister-in-law, Maria Bruno, who lived in the family home. There was also a family friend, Marinetta La Placa, who'd lived in New York City before retiring to Sicily. My family told me that I'd remember her.

There are no trains into these mountains. The bus from Cefalù clings to the Tyrrhenian coast, then begins an inland climb to the interior of the island. We are soon separated from the relatively populated and fertile coastal area. The mountains are backward and semi-barren, a region of beasts, burdens, asses and mules, occasional horses, animals so laden with sheaves of hay or grain or bundles of firewood that only their stoic heads and meager posteriors can be seen. The old men—and most of the men in Sicily are old—perched on top of these animals or leading them along are dark and sere as leather, as blank-faced as their beasts. Occasionally the patient bus would wait for a herd of sheep or goats which swept over the road from the pasture which fell off on either side.

On my first trip to Petralia I heard the people on the bus speaking a dialect identical to my grandparents'. It was a shock to hear this, the same language but in a different setting. It evoked in me a sense of belonging, and not belonging. I couldn't speak that dialect. I was so obviously different from them, a big American in Levis, towering over the women and most of the men. I was as apprehensive about that visit as I'd been about visiting Pastene, perhaps more so. There would be no way out of Petralia if the visit somehow fell through. The town had no hotel; there was no bus until the next morning. And I couldn't trust that the mail had delivered notice of my arrival. I didn't know who, if anyone, would be there to greet me. This, I thought, would be a complicated visit. There were more people. There would be factions. I'd been told that my grandparents' families had little to do with each other. My grandmother had one survivor in the town, Zia Maria, her sister-in-law, widowed for nearly forty years. And because of their isolated and probably poor living conditions, I expected them to be less pliable, and perhaps offended because I'd chosen to visit my father's people first. I'd have to perform the Italian balancing act I knew so well, giving each person equal respect and attention.

It was raining that day. Clouds hung in the deep gorges. The people riding or walking along the road had covered their heads with blankets or pieces of plastic. The bus climbed through zones of mist, zones of clear air. We passed through towns called Nicosia, Geraci, Sicula, Castelbuono, towns with streets so narrow that the bus barely squeezed through. I changed buses twice, the last time waiting at a fork in the road marked by a few bunker-like houses and a road sign: one way down, to Sottana, the other up, to Soprana. I could see neither place, only the hazed-over space between the mountains and sailing sheets of mist. Then the bus came by. It was empty. We approached Soprana by means of those interminable Italian switchbacks.

I studied the notes prepared before I left America. These were a list of relatives, some of whom I hadn't seen since I was a child, and some I couldn't remember at all. It was a condition report: those dead or alive, sick or well, those with children. I was the first bearer of news since my grandmother in 1957, and I could only hope they wouldn't ask too many questions.

The village was a stone crown on a twin-crested mountain. On the higher crest, the eastern extreme, a church's twin mosaic towers flew over the valley. The rest of the town lined up behind the church, tightly packed buildings curving down and over the lower crest. It looked like a fortress. The bus entered the concrete crown at its low point, the middle, and proceeded through rain-soaked and vacant streets to a cobblestoned piazza skirted by medieval style buildings.

I'd heard stories about people who went to Italy to find their relatives. There was always great hospitality, often humor. A friend's parents once rented a car and drove into a Sicilian town. They saw an old man sitting in the piazza smoking a cigarette. They asked directions to their uncle's house. The old man said, "I am your uncle!" The story stuck with me. In order to spare myself similar embarrassments, I'd studied photographs of my relatives before leaving America. I had some idea of what they'd look like. But when I stepped off the bus that day in Petralia I knew mistaken identity wouldn't be a problem. There was nobody there. Between the buildings I saw the haze and mountains. Around the square were unlit, unoccupied stores, and a cafe with a few men keeping out of the rain and staring at me with their blank, humorless faces. How often had they seen this before?

Then I saw that the parked bus had blocked my view. On the other side of it, at a point where a street fed into the piazza, a small group of people waited by a late model car. Who else could they be? I remembered Vittorio's son from a photograph: Angelo, a stocky redheaded fellow. Now he'd gone gray, he wore a threadbare black suit, and was the only person in black. The short and chunky women next to him wore print dresses. Youngsters filled the spaces between them. Foremost in the group, noticed last because she was so tiny, was a woman with a maroon skirt, pink shawl, and silver hair in a bun. This would be Zia Maria.

Trying to appear composed, I walked toward them across the piazza, lugging a heavy suitcase and plastic shopping bags stretched to their limits by the clinking brandy bottles I'd decided would make the best gifts. I heard *OOH's* and *AAH's* like movie audiences make

133

when a baby appears on the screen. I saw them look from me to the photograph my grandfather had sent, the "nice" photograph of the young man with shirt, tie, and jacket. When the identification was positive, the women's exclamations burst into high-pitched screeches of dialect. The old woman identified herself as Zia Maria Bruno, and teary eyed she said, *"Caro mio! Mio caro Vincenzo!"* and I understood what I meant to her, a man she'd never seen, but the only representative of a family gone from Italy and dispersed in America, a family which had forgotten her after my grandmother died in 1968.

Petralia Soprana, 1976

Petralia Soprana, 1976

My Mother's Side

Strangers aren't legion in Petralia and there hadn't been a visitor to our family since 1957. I expected to be scrutinized. I'd already been stared at in Europe; but the Sicilians, especially in the small towns, stared constantly, not with innocent curiosity because of my physical size and obviously American clothes, but with a humorless, blank hostility. My uncle Mario once jokingly predicted that if I ever went to Sicily his father's people would stare at me for days before speaking. He wasn't all wrong. My first hours in Petralia were exhausting ones because the family did so much staring. Part of our problem was language. Part was their curiosity. I was family, but I was also a foreigner who would have to be tested.

The distance from the piazza to the Giaimo house was a few hundred feet, but they insisted on driving me. My luggage was stowed in the trunk of a well-kept Simca, the women squeezed into the back, I sat up front, Angelo drove, and the youngsters walked behind us. We proceeded in low gear up a steep, thin street lined with attached and run-down houses, several of them boarded up. The Giaimo home was on the corner, near a fountain. It was a two-story cube built onto the row of neighboring houses. Like all of these it had a green door and a red tile roof with stones holding down the lowest tiles so they wouldn't blow off in the wind. There was a tiny window in front, its glass cloudy, and a larger window on the side where an open space near the fountain fell away to more channel-like streets which trickled down through the town.

Angelo and the others then presented me to Vittorio, who, as head of the family, didn't meet visitors. He received them.

A quick fellow wrapped in a scarf paced the street-level room of the house, pivoting on his cane to face me when I entered. He wore a gray cap which matched his jacket and scarf. He was taller and slimmer than my grandfather, and once redheaded. His features were delicate and birdlike, a slight hook to the nose, clear blue eyes watered over, oversized hands with their veins showing, and an air of nervous but gentle dignity. The expression on his face conveyed the importance of my visit and the intensity of his evaluation. Like Mario Panella, he was looking for family in my face. Satisfied, he greeted me with a strong hug and kiss, calling me *nipote mio* (my nephew) and trying hard to pronounce it without dialect. While he did this, his wife Giuseppina took my wet suitcase into a small pantry and began wiping the rain from it.

For the next few hours I was scrutinized like a specimen in a bottle. Their attitude was both humorous and curious as they sat me in a window seat and arranged their chairs around it as if a show was about to begin. Then they stared, simply stared, some of them smiling, some of them deadpan. The little time we'd spent together had demonstrated my non-dialect Italian, my limited vocabulary, my poor pronunciation. For those first few hours, and especially those early, excruciating minutes, we were trying to dissipate an immense curiosity, a curiosity built up over a lifetime. So they examined me as any tribe would examine a stranger—top to toe—face, body, clothing, shoes. I was doing the same, surprised to see none of the women wearing black, surprised at so many youngsters, and trying to get some grip on their dialect, which at times, and especially from the women, sounded like the screeching of birds. These were uncomfortable moments. I shrugged. They shrugged. I expected a question, a remark. None came. They kept staring, sometimes giggling like children. I began looking around the living room. The pale green walls held clusters of photographs, most of them taken in America: my grandfather, my uncles, my parents when they were together. The walls had their share of holy pictures, too, including a statue of the Virgin with tiny candle-flame bulbs beneath it.

I searched my mind for a topic I could clearly render. I saw that one of the women resembled my mother. I told her so. Everyone laughed, presumably at my Italian. I repeated the statement, slowly, with my best pronunciation. They understood. Their answer was a happy burst of dialect, like applause.

My "joke" about one of them looking like my mother had broken the ice and they began asking me questions, all of which had to be *repeated slowly*, refined, interpreted with my dictionary or by some of the youngsters familiar with formal Italian from school. They discussed my answers among themselves in rapid speech which sounded like *pitch-a-pitch-a-pitch*, not the Panella dialect with its Neapolitan elasticity, but the Giaimo dialect, southern Italian with a French and Arab cast.

The woman who resembled my mother was Vittorio's daughter, Concettina. She and Maria, (Angelo's wife,) were controlling the conversation. They wanted to know every detail of my trip, when it began, where I'd gone, who I'd seen, how much it cost. Like my family in America they could argue over these details with me, with each other. Had I taken the afternoon bus from Cefalù? Why? The morning bus was faster. Had I flown from America to Paris? Why not Palermo?

Zio Vittorio held himself apart from all this. No squabbling for him. He was still studying me, and from the way he held himself apart, and from the way they all deferred to him, it was clear that he had the respect of the family. I was the nearest he'd ever be to the brother he last saw in 1929, the brother who left home when Vittorio was five. While I spoke fitfully with the others, he'd taken out my photograph and was studying it along with a letter which someone had written for my grandfather. He showed me the letter. It was an announcement of my visit. He held it out to me as if by my recognition of it my true identity would be established. I took the letter and picture and told him they were from my grandfather. This satisfied him. He then inquired about the health of his brother and sister. He asked me about his nieces and nephews, phrasing his questions in such a way that my answers, by disclosing where they lived in America, would put another seal on his doubts.

I reported on all the relatives he asked about, giving the information remembered from my notes. When I mentioned those divorced or separated, like my aunt and mother, the women raised their cries of ill-fortune, saying, in effect, "That is the price of living in America." When I expended my information Vittorio looked at me intently, his rich blue eyes watery with tears. He told me, slowly, that he was seventy-six years old and would never see his brother again.

Silence. Zia Maria, who'd said little, clasped her hands and said,

141

"*Ma!*" This means "but" in Italian, but the word is also used to resign oneself to the world's imperfections. It is also used to punctuate moods or movements. Zia Maria rose, picked up her umbrella, and looked at me expectantly.

"When will I see you?" I asked.

The question satisfied her. The women reviewed the plans already made for my visit—where I would eat, where I would sleep, who I would visit and when. Vittorio had two sons and a daughter. All were married, all had children, and all lived in Petralia. Visits were obligatory. One of the boys wanted to show me his Vespa. The women wanted to show me their homes. I was to sleep that night and for all future visits at Concettina's house, two doors up the street.

I remained in Cefalù for nearly two months. During that time I made several trips to Petralia; and members of the Giaimo family came to visit me, usually in the two-cylinder Fiat belonging to Concettina's son. On their first visit Concettina rewashed every dish, pot, and utensil in my apartment: rented places, she said, were dirty. Only then could we eat. After dinner we would go to the beach. Those who couldn't fit into the car would walk there. I would swim, they would watch, and when it was over we would eat a *gelato* and part company after making plans for the next visit.

Vittorio Giaimo with his parents   Petralia Soprana, 1918

Vittorio Giaimo   1976

Giuseppina Giaimo   1976

ittorio and Giuseppina Giaimo   1976

Iaria Bruno   1976

Passing the Time

The *clop-clop* of a beast awoke me. From Concettina's terrace I saw a man on a mule coming up the tunnel-like street. He stopped to speak with Vittorio, who'd been sitting outside his house in a patch of sunlight. When the man rode off Vittorio resumed his trance-like attitude, looking into the sun with his eyes squinted. There was absolute silence in the town.

A chicken appeared from around a corner and proceeded down the street. Here it had as much status as a mule or a Fiat. It scanned every inch of ground. It must have walked a hundred feet without pecking a grit or a grain. My grandfather would have loved that chicken. I thought of his words. On his terms there was nothing there, only a dramatic landscape and a well-preserved culture. Things which can't be eaten. But Italians know the prices on America's menu. They remain here by choice, preferring the little they have. Vittorio lives on a small pension, whatever he can grow, whatever his children and grandchildren contribute. When not working the tiny plot of family land he sits in the street, keeping his chair against the house so an occasional car can pass.

His birthplace has outlived its function. Centuries ago Petralia needed its height for protection. Now it is a remote suburb of nothing, too rugged for large scale farming, too void of possibility to support its young men unless they are postal workers, street sweepers, or *carabinieri*. Needless to say, the town uses few of these. Except for the annual *festa* and a few high school soccer games, life is sleepy and uneventful. The main topics of conversation are the day's meal and the prices for its ingredients. Occasionally a three-wheeled truck comes up from Palermo, its driver hawking his goods from house to house, sometimes fresh vegetables, sometimes kitchenware, sometimes mattresses. Vendors sell unprocessed goat's milk in the street. In August those with wheat or dried fava beans thresh them in the public field using the ancient method: trampling with mules. The population is about three thousand, and shrinking. There are ten churches: only one is used.

The view of the towering mountains and deep valleys is available from almost every house. It enables one to see the weather. When it rains, clouds roll into the streets and the village seems to float like a ship. On fair days there is a rarefied clarity to the air. The nights are always cool. One tires easly. The piazza is a gathering place for that timeless collection of old men in black caps who sit with their elbows on their knees and, like Vittorio, stare into the distance. The cafes—there are three—are crowded when it rains, or during the *festa*, which lasts five days and is held in honor of the town's patron saints, Peter and Paul. The remainder of the town's commerce consists of a few grocery stores, a tobacco shop, one barber, one butcher, and several shoemakers who, like Vittorio once did, work from small tables in the street, or in alcoves in their homes.

Unlike Sicily's coastal towns, Petralia has cold, snowy winters, and a short growing season for the gardens which Italians depend upon so much. At this height there are no olive trees or lemon groves. Tomatoes are scarce and canned in paste form. The Giaimo family preserves them in soda or wine bottles sealed with an inch or so of olive oil. The paste is precious. The pastina for my first dinner was flavored with a little olive oil and parsley, then mixed with a few drops of tomato paste shaken from the bottle like catsup. Not everybody took some. Vittorio's fine, ruby-colored wine is taken sparingly as well.

In Petralia, as in much of southern Italy, water is rationed, turned on each morning and available until people use up the daily supply, which is usually gone before noon. Modernized homes like Concettina's have reservoir tanks on their roofs. Many houses have no plumbing at all. Water must be drawn from the public fountains, which run continuously until the town's daily ration is used up.

The church at the higher end of town is called the Chiesa di Loreto. Its twin spires are coated with multicolored mosaics, and historians would probably describe it as a Norman-French church

148

with Arab influences. The Giaimo family knows nothing of these matters. They only know the church is no longer used. Its doors are opened once a year, during the festa, when its larger-than-life statues are mounted on wooden platforms, adorned with flowers and candles, and paraded through the streets on the shoulders of the townsmen. Since I attended the festa, I was able to enter the church. The triple-domed interior was bright white and light-flooded, but its walls and ceilings had peeled from lack of ventilation.

A belvedere, or terrace with a view, is part of the church. It affords a vista of most of the countryside around and below the village. In the valley and lower mountains are clusters of homes, the hump-shaped mountaintop town of Gangi, a salt mine, and a small cement plant. Men and mules work the small wheat fields, goats and sheep graze along the roads. A footpath runs crookedly down to a grotto where a glass-covered picture of the Virgin peers out from the rocks and flowers.

The *festa* celebrating the town's patron saints is held in late June and is the grand event of the year. Colored lights are strung between the buildings, carnival rides are brought in, and the streets echo with American pop music. It is a time for out-of-towners. Tourists, unaware that some streets are too narrow for large cars, cause traffic jams, often in front of Vittorio's house. Vendors set up tents and booths to sell a variety of goods: clothing, cloth, watches, records, tapes, kitchen equipment, accessories for domestic animals, and hand tools for the kind of small scale farming prevalent in Petralia. On the first evening there is a parade in which young boys carry half-size statues of Saints. Peter and Paul through the streets. The procession begins and ends at the church, and is led by small children carrying paper lanterns and burning sheaves of wheat. The statues are decorated with fresh flowers and battery-powered lights, and they are followed through the streets by a loud band, clergy, *carabinieri*, and the townspeople, who walk arm in arm and talk casually. After the procession everyone gathers in the piazza. The band plays several rousing songs. A group of young people then sing a praise to Peter and Paul. At the end of the song a bass drum beats loud and fast and those holding the statues rush them back into the church with much whistling and clapping from the crowd. On the fifth night the statues of Peter and Paul are life size, and are accompanied by all the saint statues from the Chiesa di Loreto.

149

After the procession there is a fireworks display, and several hours of music. These last are the highlights of the festa. The piazza is choked with people sitting on the church steps, or in chairs carried from home. The fireworks are loud, and the music lasts until long after midnight. It is mixed music, performed by glee clubs, soloists, and rock groups; but, being music, it is a treat in itself, and the people enjoy all of it

Like my grandfather, Vittorio could separate work from rest, doing nothing when it was time to do nothing, "passing the time," as my grandfather liked to put it. If I wanted to sit with Vittorio in the street, Giuseppina (called Peppina) would bring me a chair and he would make sure I sat clear of any possible traffic. He is a careful man with no apparent appetite for irregular events, a man who thinks first and foremost of having enough to eat. He doesn't read and will have nothing to do with politics. Once at dinner while talking about the upcoming Italian elections with his grandson—who appeared to be conservative—Vittorio cut short the discussion. The dining-room windows were open and he didn't want the neighbors to hear. His grandson deferred to his wish and we continued the discussion outside the house.

Vittorio talked about his family in America with a sense of loss and puzzlement. He explained that because he was too young to travel he'd been left behind by his sister and two brothers, who went away and promised to return. His job had been to watch the house and take care of the parents. The promises to return were never kept. My grandfather made a visit with my uncle Angelo in 1929. Their gift to Vittorio had been to install electricity in the house. That was the last time the brothers saw each other. With the exception of the packages, which stopped years ago, and Christmas cards with sketchy news and a little money, Vittorio had become the forgotten brother. Several years before my visit he received a note saying that his other brother had died. There were no details. He felt powerless to control any of these events, and he knew he was permanently cut off from his remaining brother and sister.

He made a life in Petralia as a shoemaker, setting up his table in the street or his vestibule, working for cash or for goods and services. The table is still there, covered up, *in riposo*, as he emphatically put it, uncovered only for family repairs. Peppina was an orphan from a home near Palermo, and together they had three children.

150

All of them lived in Petralia. Angelo and Concettina live on the same street, Salvatore lives near the piazza. Like most of my Sicilian relatives in America, the children have safe, modest goals. Concettina, whose husband worked in Germany for twelve years, is content with a modern house, three working sons, and the husband who has been a good if absent provider. Angelo works where he can find it, sometimes in construction, sometimes in the fields with his father-in-law: his pay is a share of the wheat. Salvatore, the youngest and more sophisticated son, worked in Germany for two years, then lost an eye in an accident with an air hammer. He returned to Petralia and opened a small store where he sells and repairs shoes.

Vittorio is the center of the family. He carries himself that way, both modestly and with power. He sits in front of his house while his children and grandchildren come to him. He and Peppina take their meals with Concettina. I saw no sign of dissatisfaction with his children. He seemed to make few judgments. Two grandsons are named Vittorio, two granddaughters Giuseppina.

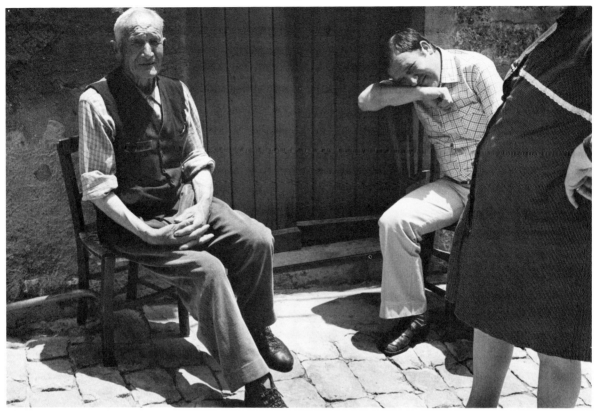

Vittorio with his grandson in front of the Giaimo home

Boy picking peas

Giuseppina Giaimo

Bumper cars

Threshing wheat

The Beast in the Basement

The animals were the most significant sign that so little had changed in Petralia. They were a key part of the economy. Herds passed through the streets. Men on donkeys led pairs of goats behind them. Once from Salvatore's terrace I watched two boys galloping their sleek mules through the cobblestoned streets. As a boy I was puzzled when they told me that my grandfather delivered bread with a horse and wagon. What did he know about horses?

Vittorio's donkey is stabled in the basement of his house. Sometimes he tethers it in La Pinta, the public field. He rides it quarter saddle, but without a saddle, both legs hanging over the animal's left shoulder. He controls it with a kind of hackamore, no bit, just a halter with a serrated nose grip. He called the donkey his Signorina. The dialect word for donkey is *assicareddu*. People shorten and change the second syllable, calling the animal *la shake*. During the festa when the town was crowded with visitors, mostly from Palermo (bad reputation), Vittorio locked the *shake* in the basement. Most of the old-timers, and the town is mostly old-timers, keep animals in their basements. The houses were designed for that. In America we didn't believe my grandfather when he told us where they kept the donkey.

I love you

ai love iou

j are you going t

ar you coing tu

Dialect

Italy is a nation of provinces, and no provincial difference is more apparent than dialect. While studying Italian, I began to see the connection between the heavy Sicilian dialect spoken at home and the "proper" Italian taught in the schools. Only then did I learn how to spell the words and phrases that my grandparents' dialect had altered. In so doing I became less self-conscious about using the language. My first Italian instructor was Bolognese, and his regional speech was textbook perfect. I discovered while reciting in class that I had a built-in tendency to use dialect pronunciation. He was politely amused by this, which is to say that he revealed a measure of condescension.

Pretension toward language exists in Italy as elsewhere. But a dialect reflects history, not vulgar deviation. Prior to the unification of Italy in 1860, Sicily had been controlled by Africans, Greeks, Romans, Germans, French, and Spanish. Some of these conquering tribes and nations only managed to control part of the island, thus preserving pockets of dialect which remain intact today. The dialect spoken by the Giaimo family is characterized by a musical, Arabic sound. They tend, for example, to place vowels before and after words and phrases. They will not simply say a word like *Soprana*; they will say *a-Soprana*.

What frustrated me in Sicily was that I knew the sound of it, like music from my youth. I knew short phrases and discrete words, but I couldn't construct sentences. As I made more visits to Petralia and as the Giaimo family came down to Cefalù, there was an accomodation: we adjusted to each other's Italian. In the two months I spent in Sicily, often in Cefalù where Sicilians can speak more formally, my Italian became fairly proficient. I had no problem communicating. But I was never able to speak their dialect.

They could always lose me when they broke into dialect, at least during the early part of my stay. And they had the habit I knew from home—especially the women—of speaking in rapid dialect when my part of the conversation was neither wanted nor needed. Once at dinner they remarked among themselves that I didn't make the sign of the cross before eating. When I announced that their remark had been understood, they asked me to explain it. When I did they were embarrassed.

Dialects depart from formal Italian in varying degrees, the further south in Italy the closer to Sicilian. Generally, and in Petralia as well, the dialect contains numerous vocabulary changes and a severe modification in pronunciation. But the rules of pronunciation are consistent. Take formal Italian, elongate vowels, soften consonants, and eliminate the articles *la* and *lo*: these are replaced with *a* and *u*. My grandmother didn't make *la pizza*: she made *a-beets*. The word for beautiful, *bella*, becomes *bedda*. The onion, *la cipolla*, is *a cibudda*. Knife, *coltello*, is *corderdu*. Peas, *piselli*, are *piseddi*. The pronoun him, *lui*, is *iddu*. The Neapolitan word for "up there," *angoppa*, is *dancappo*. Its opposite, "down there," is *giù* in Naples and most of Italy, *dug* in Sicily. The directional word there, *là* in formal Italian, is *da* in the south. Thus "There he is!" is said as "Da è iddu!" For a north-to-south overview, the phrase "this here" is *questa qui* in Florence, *questa qua* in Rome and Naples, and *cheesta cha* in Petralia Soprana.

Prices and Aspirations

They wake up early to get their share of the water. When it begins to flow they fill their sinks and bathtubs, pots and bottles. With some economizing it will last the day. By 6 A.M. Vittorio has taken his post in the sunny part of the street. Concettina is starting dinner. When I come downstairs her first words are *"Acqua c'e!"* if there is running water, or *"Acqua non c'e!"* if there is none.

In America we'd call her pushy. She is the most salient Giaimo child, forceful and manipulative, more so than the good-natured Angelo or the aloof Salvatore. She is chief of hospitality, scheduling my trips, arranging cheaper departures to Cefalù or Palermo, and stretching my visits a day or two despite my protests. She cooks all my meals—except those taken with Zia Maria—and like Mario and Esterina Panella, she constantly forced second and third helpings on me. I gave in to most of this, knowing it stemmed from a desire to please. But one day I refused a third helping of *pasta al forno*. She put it on my plate anyway. I slid it back to the serving dish. She tried again. I put it back once again. Then I said in crisp Italian, "One must live his own life." I might have fired a pistol. Dead silence settled over the dozen of us at the table. Some stilted explanations and apologies followed. Concettina was hurt, but we'd reached an understanding. Some days later she was able to joke about it, and even asked to have a photo taken in which she forced me to eat while I refused.

She was covetous of my company, always wanting to know my whereabouts if I left her house, and letting me know if she approved of where I'd gone. For my first visits I could never walk alone in the town. If I set off by myself she would either interrupt her work to come along or send one of the youngsters after me. This, like the forcing of food, was well meant, the protective dimension of her hospitality. She didn't want me to get into a situation beyond the limits of my Italian. When she walked with me, she insisted that we lock arms. She introduced me to her friends; she led me past her enemies, holding herself obviously erect and proud. After a few visits I had to insist on walking alone: they gave in.

They took pride in their hospitality. I was certain that in Petralia, even more than in Pastene, meals were more elaborate than what the family was used to. Pasta was always accompanied by meat and cheese courses. There was always fresh fruit; always an insistence that I take second and third helpings. *"Mangiasti?"* Have I eaten? They tried to conceal their poor circumstances and to give me the best, no, better than they had to offer. But their economic condition was difficult to conceal. Soon I became aware of their intense and solemn discussion of food prices, their spare eating habits: breakfast was a puddle of coffee in the bottom of a cup, with *biscotti* when I was there, but with nothing, I'm sure, when I wasn't. They never made a frivolous purchase. I once asked Vittorio, the teen-age boy, to have a cup of coffee with me in the cafe. He stoutly refused, During the festa I watched Maria buy a pair of shears from a vendor by first offering a low price: when this was refused, angrily, as if it were an insult, she coupled the shears with a second item and made another offer which would have netted her the shears for the same price. The offer was accepted.

I slept at Concettina's house, the most modern. Her bedroom looked like Mario Panella's: the bed large and fastidiously made, the walls hung with vivid pictures and relics. I was told by Salvatore and Angelo that on my next visit to Italy I could stay with them because their houses would be ready for guests by then.

Concettina was the only Giaimo with running water in the home. Her house had been resurfaced on the outside and finished on the inside with paneled walls, marble floors, and matching furniture in some of the rooms. It was a modern home by any standard, with this exception: Concettina avoided using her appliances. During the day she worked in a darkened kitchen; her water heater and automatic washer were rarely used; most laundry was done by hand.

They are hard people to know, ingenuous at times, self-conscious

164

of their circumstances, secretive about their possessions, covetous of my loyalty, but more prepared to be hospitable, I think, than my family in America would be. But their focus on survival has cut certain responses. Despite their warmth and their almost immediate acceptance of me, I sensed in them a cold, untouchable core, a cauterized zone in the area of their frugality and resignation. Life had them trapped in its coarser sieves, in the details: they argued over prices, not aspirations. These have been cut from the lives of the older people, clipped in the youngsters. Young Vittorio spoke with forced enthusiasm about an assembly line job at the new Fiat plant in Termini Imerese, a nearby city. But the obstacles seemed great, and probably were: competition and transportation. The law prohibits his Vespa on the autostrada.

When I saw the old men sitting in the piazza, I wondered if they were content or sullen: I concluded the latter. They not only sat there. They smoked and looked at the ground, or stared at strangers with blank, dark eyes. Vittorio spent as much time sitting as they did, but he seemed different from them, as if the sun would be enough. As a contrast I'd watched Salvatore in the piazza, leaning against a building and scanning with his good eye. He had a way of hanging back and watching everything: a man with a secret. I visited him at "work" one day. He was sitting outside his store. The buildings around him were covered with political posters for the right, left, and center. Salvatore's store had no sign to advertise its purpose. With a sign, he said, he would have to pay taxes. Inside the store the lights were off. There was a small repair table like his father's, but no work on it. Boxes of shoes were stacked from floor to ceiling. We sat in the store for over an hour, hearing the banal ticking of the clock in the quiet spaces between our subjects of conversation. He spoke of politics with absolute cynicism. No form of government could help him, or Italy. He covered the other routes with surprising speed: the realignment of world prices for raw materials as one source of Italy's problem, the need for people to rethink their way of living. Then the conversation ran aground once again. I left, wondering about the outlets for his sophistication.

Giuseppina's kitchen

Concettina's bedroom

The Giaimo family, Petralia Soprana, 1976

Concettina Giaimo La Placa

Maria Giaimo

Angelo and Giuseppina Giaimo

Giuseppina and Vittorio Giaimo

Vittorio La Placa

Giuseppina Giaimo

Salvatore Giaimo

The Widows

We'd been told about Zia Maria only when my mother and grand-mother judged us mature enough. After his marriage to Maria, my grandmother's brother, Leonardo, joined the army and contracted syphilis in a brothel. In his fear and ignorance, he did nothing about the disease. It was transferred not to his wife, but to his daughter. He died of it. The child, Concettina, contracted it when she began to menstruate. She died in 1936 after a long illness. Zia Maria has lived the life of a penitent since then, an object of condescension by the Giaimo family, and of more bitter scorn by Leonardo's stepmother, Mamma Grande, who wanted to take the Bruno house away from Maria after the child died. But my grand-mother wouldn't let Maria pay for Leonardo's sins. She persuaded the children of her brother Paul in America not to sign their share of the house over to Mamma Grande, and she paid to keep the house in repair over the years. Today it belongs to Zia Maria.

As she so often reminded me during my visits, Zia Maria was alone. "*Sono sola, una vedova,*" she'd say, clasping her hands in a gesture of futile prayer. But she was right. Unlike Vittorio, she is neither mother nor grandmother to a large family arriving daily to pay its respects. What remains of her family is in Messina, and they rarely visit. Some second and third cousins in Petralia see to her wood and water and share their garden with her. Otherwise she lives on her husband's pension (he was a postman) and earnings from sewing or crocheting fine cotton lace, work she does less and less as her eyes grow poorer.

But she isn't completely alone. Her somewhat constant companion is Marinetta La Placa, my grandmother's closest Italian friend in New York, and also a native of Petralia. She was widowed less than a year after she and her husband returned from America to retire. Now she is the foil to Maria's pessimism and fatalistic philosophizing.

To be a member of an Italian family is never to be simply yourself. You are perceived as part of some faction in a major family dispute. To the widows I was an extension of my grandmother, their ally. I was to be sympathetic to their side in the old war against Mamma Grande for ownership of the house. At the time of my visit Mamma Grande was still alive, over one hundred years old and living in a rest home in America. Marinetta, who knew my family back home, also saw me as the son of the Neapolitan, whom she also knew.

"Whatsa matter?" she said when I entered Zia Maria's house for my appointed dinner. "You no remember me?"

Did I? That raspy, aggressive voice was a reminiscent prelude to all the twisted ears and smacks in the face I'd received as a boy from various elders. The face behind her glasses was a grandmother's face, but there was nothing soft about it. I knew it, though. On the perimeter of my memory I saw our basement in Queens, where my grandmother cooked and this woman sat, like a steel judge, a tiny cup of coffee in front of her, sharp, explosive dialect crowding the room. She was my grandmother's letter writer, adviser, and advocate, especially during the struggle to keep Zia Maria in the Bruno house. When she spoke to me in those days and I wouldn't reply, she'd say, *"Whatsa matta you no gabeesha 'dalian?"* Then my indifferent shrug.

"I remember you," I said.

"You tell your mother she's no good because she no write! They forget us over here! They no do right!"

I agreed with her. We had forgotten them. But I couldn't speak for everyone in my family, and I couldn't repair previous neglect. The strength and cohesion in my family had certainly been weakened since my grandmother's death, to judge by poor Zia Maria. Everything about her spelled loneliness. Her living room was nearly bare, the furniture worn out. Her wall decorations were a shrine to the Virgin and a blown-up family picture with her dead husband

174

and lost daughter. The view from her window was that vast, hazed-over space, and those ghostly green and purple mountains.

Zia Maria clasped her hands and apologized for her humble home, referring to the will of God, her widowhood, her poverty. But Marinetta cut her off sharply by winking at me and saying, "Come on, we eat upstairs."

The top floor of the house was the kitchen, a thin room with a wood-fired stove no longer in use. All cooking was done on a small, bottled gas burner. Together the widows served up eggplant appetizer, pasta, veal, chewy bread, salad, and a strong wine. They took little for themselves. There was the usual forcing of food. After the meal while we cut fruit, Marinetta said, "We're surprised that your great-grandmother is still alive," referring to Mamma Grande. I explained that I hadn't seen my great-grandmother in many years, long before she went to the rest home. I added that my Aunt Katie made regular visits to the home, but that I knew nothing of her condition. Marinetta dropped the subject with a passive shrug of the shoulders. So much for an enemy. We turned to other issues. For the second time in Petralia I went down the list of people in America she might know, the marriages, divorces, jobs, children, and the delicate subject of my parents. Marinetta sympathized with her own.

"How come you no speak with your father?"

"What should I say to him?"

"You tell him to get back with your mother."

"This is their business."

"The misery your grandma went through over that man."

We turned again to the subject of my family's neglect of their Italian relatives. I could make no excuses, but I wondered why they'd cut themselves off from their past. Probably because they found it too difficult to explain that America had subverted the old culture in the span of two generations. In Petralia that culture was intact. For better or for worse, how could my family explain their changes to relatives in Italy?

175

Maria and Concettina Bruno   Petralia Soprana, 1920

Maria Bruno   1976

Maria Bruno and Marinetta La Placa   1976

Marinetta La Placa   1976

Home

Early one morning with my luggage and gifts I sat in the Chevrolet van which makes a weekday run from Petralia to Palermo via several hill towns. In the street by Concettina's house the Giaimo family and Zia Maria were waving goodbye, a gesture executed in Italy like the American "come here." I returned to New York by way of Zurich, a city so organized compared to Italy it seemed lobotomized. I arrived home like a true tourist, laden with goods: Sicilian pottery, lace from Zia Maria, a jug of Vittorio's wine, a bag of strong Sicilian oregano stuffed into my boot.

My grandfather was ninety years old then, and aging fast. He was arthritic. His eyesight was poor. He could barely make out the photographs. Slides on the big screen were better. Without realizing he was blocking the light from the projector, he would stand up to point something out. But he recognized the old landmarks, and he was sentimental about them as he'd never been before.

My father kept his metal exterior. He looked at the photographs of his cousin, his house, his father's clock in the church tower. He ate the nutted chocolates from Benevento. He said, "Did they ever pave the street in that town?"

We compared notes about Pastene: what he remembered, what I saw. We spoke about his cousin's way of life. But we were still talking around the subject. I was trying to convey the beauty of his birthplace, and my understanding of what he'd left behind. He knew it. But he still preferred his comic wall. So we kept the subject of Italy on a more comfortable basis, talking about the prices Italians pay for gasoline, coffee, meat.

"Those Italians," he said. "They had Libya. They were walking on top of all that oil and didn't know it."

Jenny's death had pulled him and Sylvia even closer together. During my trip to Italy they had witnessed more bitter evidence that members of their family died young. My father now spoke with Sylvia every day, and if he couldn't reach her, he entered her apartment with a passkey.

In the spring of 1978 Sylvia was hospitalized for pneumonia. It was cured. On the day of her release she had a stroke, went into a long coma, then died. She was sixty-seven. "I don't know why we are so unlucky but all of us die young," wrote Mario Panella. Sylvia had been living alone in a condominium near my father, and near Jenny's son, Vincent, who'd promised his mother to watch after her sister. She was a childless widow, and after Jenny's death a grand aunt and grandmother to all the Panellas of my generation and the generations after. She was a Panella above all, with a harder, more merciless brass than either of her brothers or her sister. She was outspoken, opinionated, a believer in single causes, a great story-teller, an opera lover, and protector of my father, for whom no woman could be too good. But she was lonely in her last years, her fixed income preventing travel to Italy. Her neighbors were "senior citizens," and she didn't like that flavor. She'd been talking about a move to Florida, but she'd become despondent, writing only two letters to Italy in two years, saying to Mario, "I haven't written, not because I don't think of you, but because I don't know where to begin." Mario understood that Jenny was the strong female figure in the family: after her death, Sylvia began losing the energy to make changes in her own life.

My father and I have reached parity and steady state. Until later in life I was blind to his limitations. He made me feel as if I was full of them. Now that war is over. He knows I can't be changed. I know he isn't always right. When he visits me I acquaint him with my labor: the room, books, papers, typewriter, the schedule. Now he encourages me. He can visualize my work setting, something he'd been unable to do during my years away from home.

Less than two months after Sylvia's death my grandfather died in Angelo's arms. He was nearly ninety-two. His last months had been painful. The wake was held in the funeral parlor on Woodside Avenue which had become a family fixture over the years, used for

Uncle Frank, my grandmother, then my grandfather. Several neighbors from Tenth Avenue attended. Some were natives of Petralia. I discovered distant cousins of my generation who'd been there. Our experiences were similar: the suffocating attention, the proud hospitality, the spare life. It was a social funeral, my grandfather looking little different from when I last saw him alive—peaceful, resting, no longer the robust man of steady labor. I thought that his death caused less grief because his life could be clearly perceived. He was what he seemed to be. One of my grandmother's nephews told me how the bread business had helped all of them through the Depression years; how he "ran bread for Uncle Pete" for a few pennies a day, not for the pay but for a chance to drive the horse. So in my thirty-eighth year I had another look at the people who'd puzzled me, the serious men and the ladies in black. They were considerably more Americanized. In fact, very few wore black. Their English was better, too. When they spoke Italian they didn't lose me, and this time I didn't mind the kisses.

Mortality restores our sense of balance. I can punctuate my life-long obsession with my family by those funerals. Limousines, flowers, mass cards, the rites in which the church tries to fill the void with the dream that God will, in Isaiah's words, "destroy death." I grope for the family dead, see them being born, walking on top of the earth, sailing over the ocean, baking bread, selling whiskey, cringing, fighting, scheming, making babies and money, propelling offspring like me into new and ironic arenas. The last two to die were neighbors on Tenth Avenue but they were as different as night and day. My Sicilian grandfather rarely mentioned Sylvia. And she never spoke of him except to remark that she had a hard time understanding his dialect. Now they will blend into my history.

Wakes are shorter than they used to be as funeral parlors stream-line their operations. During off hours we went to Sylvia's apartment with its baroque fittings, or to the pine-paneled basement of my grandfather's house. There we sat down to platters of Italian cold cuts, long loaves of bread, beer, whiskey, wine, veal, ziti, and a great deal of talk: moot points, some teary memories, and stories about the dead when they were living.

Across the Alley from
the Alamo

Mario cooks breakfast upstairs, where my mother's family lives. He uses the gold and blue Magic Chef stove from Thirty-third Street, the place where I was born but don't remember. "I make the best eggs in the world," he says. "The best!" He does, too. He uses butter instead of bacon fat and he flips them high. He catches them without breaking the yolks, which come out pink. The whites are never crusty. Soon everyone is up and moving around. There is a burst of Italian. It sets off other bursts. I figure out what's going on by hands and attitudes. Grandpa's mad because Mario uses too much butter. Grandma sides with Mario. Uncle Willie tells Grandpa that he's been to houses where they're not cheap with food. Uncle Angelo wants everyone to be quiet. My grandmother begins to laugh and comes behind me. She presses my cheeks with her hands and says a word which means "handsome." My grandfather looks at the ceiling and curses in Italian.

It is Saturday and Mario will take me to the beach. I eat my egg with a toasted slice of Silvercup bread and think of Rockaway. The word clatters and rolls, like the roller coaster, like the waves. Mario said if I rode it once I wouldn't be afraid any more. I rode it once. He reminded me that I was once afraid of the water, too. I was. My mother or Aunt Katie would carry me into the ocean and jump with the high, briny waves, holding my head just above the swelling water. I would cry at the feeling of weightlessness. They would laugh. But when Mario did it I didn't cry. First he held me up to the small waves so the water broke against my chest. Then he held me in bigger waves. Then he'd let me go and make me dog-paddle to him. After that he taught me how to "ride the waves." He always knew the right expressions for things. "Ride the waves, Jim! Ride the waves!" He called me Jim; it was my grandfather's nickname too. He knows the rules for all the games. In handball he tells me to wait until the ball is near the ground before hitting it. Then I can make a "killer." When we throw a baseball together he tells me to be a pitcher: they make the most money. He tells me about fighting. I am to fight dirty if I have to. With a brick, a rock, a stick, with the top of a garbage can. I am to kick and bite. I must never lose. I am to pick up the nearest thing and use it. "Remember, Jim, the nearest thing. I don't care what it is."

Everyone is going to the beach. The small streets are emptying their cars into Queens Boulevard, Woodhaven Boulevard, then Rockaway Boulevard. The farther we go, the more traffic we meet. I am squeezed into the back seat of my father's 1940 Nash, between two women, American women. The radio plays the same song over and over:

> Across the alley from the Alamo,
> A pinto pony and a Navajo . . .

America pleases me. Remember the Alamo, the cowboys, the Indians, the alley. The alley I knew. The rest I would grow into. Mario is driving. His boisterous friends are drinking take-out beer from cardboard cups. The perfumy women call me "doll" and say they wish I was older. Rewards appear on my horizon. It never strikes me that I go with the car. Soon I smell salt water, hear the WHOOSH! that is both ocean and roller coaster, then the voices screaming in unison as the coaster plunges. We park near Rockaway Playland and walk across the hot, splintery boardwalk. If Mario has money I will get waffles and ice cream. If Mario has money everything is possible.

The woman with Uncle Mario will become my Aunt Dolores. She is Irish. She took my sister for a roller-coaster ride while I waited near the ticket booth, watching the car through the rickety lattice-work. I said Hail Marys as fast as I could. The next week Dolores took me on. "Remember to scream," she said. I was too scared to open my mouth. "Scream!" she cried, as we topped the first hump.

186

We dropped. I screamed and the fear flew out of me.

Mario takes me places. Softball games in the Long Island league he plays in (batting cleanup). Dodger games, Ranger games, Football-Giant games. He is always betting. He and his friends don't play sports in the P.S. 69 schoolyard unless it's for money. Dollar a man, two dollars a man, five dollars a man. He plays blackjack on the steps and craps against the handball court wall, the dice going *chick-a-chick-a-chick* in his fist, the exchange of bills and bets impossible for me to follow. "Come here, Jim," he said once while he was standing in the crowd playing craps. "What kind of pants do you have on?" He pulled at my pocket. I wondered what he wanted. Then I found two dollars there. One day we went to the delicatessen on Thirty-seventh Avenue and bought roast pork sandwiches on Italian bread with salt, pepper, and mayonnaise. He gave me mine and said, "This is called a *Hero*, a *Guinea Hero*."

Near the end of grade school I joined a gang. It was our turn to rule the schoolyard. Mario and his friends had gone into the bars. We played fewer sports. I was the reader in the crowd, the self-appointed sage and joker. During that period I could never resolve the complex equation consisting of the heroism I knew from books, my mean-spirited behavior, and my need to identify with something. I floated. During the week I rode a dreary subway to school; on weekends I drank with my friends. We barely used the city, preferring the predictability of the neighborhood. We were too rude for girls. Sex was furtive, dating unheard of. During this time my father tried to reach me by admitting, for the first time, that he had a problem: he was afraid I would follow my friends, who were waiting to quit school and work, or to volunteer for the military service. It was one of the few times he tried to change his stance with me. But I was sullen and angry over his restrictions. I felt that he owed me my rowdy freedom since I'd kept my promise to stay in school.

He had what he called a "gin mill" on South Street called The Marine Bar and Grill. Over the years he would take me there as a way of spending time with me. All my Sicilian uncles had worked there before the family became divided, and it was a lucrative business until the 1950s, when the South Street piers were closed as part of the Battery Park expansion. It became a wino bar, with a walkdown ramp, sawdust on the floor, and a broken Wurlitzer with 78 rpm records. The main drink sold was muscatel, by the bottle or water glass. As a boy I wasn't allowed inside. I would sit in the car and watch the ragged, festering men waiting for my father to open the doors. In winter these men went hatless, coatless, and often without socks. They were able to endure the cold because the alcohol had destroyed their nerve endings. Their heads were often bandaged because the police beat them and took their money. As a teen-ager I was allowed to help clean up the bar on Sundays, and sometimes to sit at the bar, where the men would defer to me because of my father and tell me how they'd been doomed by drink. These men constantly praised my father's honesty. One of them showed me his bankbook and passport, which my father kept behind the bar. When he needed money to drink, my father gave it to him. When it was time to sober up, my father would cut him off. But these and other stories did little to change my attitude: my father was too absent, too authoritarian. I felt that our trips to The Marine Bar were contrived object lessons.

At home we ate spaghetti, snails, clams, fish, pizza, lambs' heads split open and roasted with their eyes and brains still in. On Thanksgiving lasagne came before the turkey. My grandmother could cook anything. She liked to make chicken soup on Monday and say, "It washes away the sins of the weekend." Sometimes on Christmas or New Year's my father would get drunk and cry in her arms. It was frightening when I first saw it.

When she died my grandfather took it very hard. At the wake he cried so much they called the priest for an extra visit. After consoling my grandfather privately, he gave the rest of us a speech. He said that my grandmother had left the world and now sat in heaven next to God. That was a mistake. It violated my grandfather's sense of reality. He stood up and cried, "Is no true! She's right here! She's dead!"

The house in Queens has been improved over the years, but the yard has suffered since my grandmother's day. She kept two peach trees, a pair of fig trees, and a wall of flowers along the driveway. Next to the garage and vegetable garden is a kind of gazebo with trellised sides and a conical roof, the site for birthday parties and outdoor picnics. This is all in obvious symbolic decay now, the tiny party house caked with city grit, the peach trees dead and cut down, the remaining fig tree tended faithfully by Angelo. The driveway is cemented over. The downstairs apartment where we lived is rented to a man who locks himself in. The sense of openness created by the presence of two connected families is gone.

The basement, finished by my father when he still owned half the house, was the dining room for both families. Here Willie and Mario teased their father about being cheap. Here Angelo tried to exert his influence on his younger brothers. Here also my relatives played high stakes poker games, a crucial hand or two of which my grandfather could recount until the time of his death, card by card: "*I gotta two ace, beck 'n' beck.*" I looked on, ran out for cake and cigars, served coffee, slyly allowed my more generous uncles to slip money into my hand. I read their lives by the way they played. Grandpa Giaimo was steady and safe, never bluffing, and often winning modestly. Willie played like his father, but he won less often. Mario, the youngest, the man who would bake bread with gas, was a reckless bettor, either winning or losing heavily. Uncle Al, Sylvia's husband, was a hard luck player. I saw him win a decisive hand only once: he drew four threes, but the pot was small because all the players hadn't arrived. Frank was cursed with good cards but few winning hands. It was my father who played with an aggressive, diverting chatter, a little brass, a little bluff, and the ability to talk the cards right out of the deck, or at least make people believe he could.

They were fresh from Tenth Avenue then, into the high gear of their lives. My father was running bars; Frank and Willie had Smiley's Express; Mario was moving from job to job: the docks, the railroad yard, Smiley's. They were yet to surrender their dreams to me. I knew almost nothing about their past then, and when they tried to tell me, I wouldn't listen. These are the family truths we bear, no matter how much we come to know.

189

MOM - MARIO - FARM -

EMIL'S PACKARD wow